What Would Washington

A Story About

Stephen H Kellogg

David G Katz

Table of Contents

Dedication

This book is dedicated to Capt. David M Davies, US Army, deceased, who was billeted in my previous room when it was blown up April 1, 1966, to his surviving family and all those brave Americans I served with in Vietnam.

Acknowledgments

I'd like to say thank you to my beautiful wife, Rosalind and
my loving family who encouraged me to write this book,
and thank the following friends who have in some way
helped and supported me through this journey: Michael
Enzinger, Adam Boyer, Tony, and Angela Amadore, Dave
Schaeffer, Rusty Morgan, and Isabel Chason. And thank
you to my Creator for giving me a full life and the
opportunity to write this book.

About the Author

The author was born in Providence, Rhode Island, and spent most of his youth growing up there, graduating from the University of Rhode Island with a BS in Accounting and as a commissioned ROTC Officer. Weeks after graduation, he began his military service in the 2nd Armored Division and served in Vietnam one year later. After returning home, he married his childhood sweetheart and worked for a public accounting firm and then a small equities firm before founding three businesses over his next 40 years before retiring. He started his music career at 16 and now enjoys performing alone or with one of his musical groups around Atlanta, Georgia, which he now calls home. This is his first novel, a work of fiction, and written after retiring when the time was right.

Prologue

They were gone now. Jason's wife Jean, his daughter Susan and his son-in-law, Mike. He stood over their graves, staring, thinking, eyes tearing. He was still in shock. In an instant, his whole world ended. How could it be? When the sobbing faded away, silence came. Soon after, the memories of Jean showed up in Jason's mind, and all he wanted to do was re-live those beautiful times.

Part One: The Beginning

Chapter I

The call came in just before noon. Jason and Jean drove to the hospital with all smiles, singing along with their favorite music blasting inside Molly. They arrived to find Mike in the waiting area while Susan was in the delivery room.

"She's right on time," Mike said, "it was a little scary driving here because I thought I wouldn't make it in time, but all is well, and she's really close to delivering our new son."

Jean hugged Mike, then Jason hugged Mike and said, "So she's alright then?"

"Oh yeah!" replied Mike, "She's holding up like a champ."

They all sat down in the waiting area, smiling with great anticipation, and shortly thereafter, the nurse arrived to inform Mike that he was the proud father of a healthy baby boy. They exploded with cheers while the nurse explained that Susan was doing just fine and it would be only a matter of time before she and the baby could have visitors. Mike asked Jason if he would like to join him to smoke a cigar outside the hospital as a male tradition, even though neither one had ever smoked before. So there they were, standing on the hospital sidewalk, coughing their heads off and laughing at each other with joy. After visiting with Susan and seeing the baby, Jason departed while Jean and Mike stayed with Susan. The following day Jean called Jason to inform him that Susan and the baby were doing just fine and that the four of them would be leaving the hospital tomorrow afternoon and would call as soon as they arrived at their home.

The next day, a little after 2:00 PM, Jason's cell phone rang with Jean's name showing on his phone. He answered the phone with excitement, but once he heard the unfamiliar voice coming from the other end, his face turned red, and his mind became confused.

"Mr. Jason Davies?" the voice said.

"Yes?" he answered.

"Sir, my name is Sargent Owens, with the county police. Are you the spouse of Jean Davies?"

"Yes" is all Jason could think of to say.

"And are you related to Mr. and Mrs. Mike Kellogg?

"Yes, but what's this all about?" questioned Jason.

"Sir, I'm calling you from the hospital. There's been an accident involving your family, and I was wondering if you could come over to the hospital as soon as you can."

"Is everyone all right?"

"Sir, the baby is fine. Could you please come to the hospital so we can explain everything we know?"

"Well…well, well yes, but…" the line went dead.

He got strapped into his 'sunmobile', turned on the vehicle's battery, gave verbal instructions to 'Molly, the mobile voice', and off he went. His usual drive was manual. He enjoyed the control of the wheel and the feeling of rubber on the road, but he knew his emotions were flying everywhere, so he prudently let Molly do the driving. His thoughts were racing, one after the other, until he finally arrived at the emergency room. Thirty minutes after he left his home, he approached the entrance to the hospital emergency room, which was packed with cars, ambulances, gurneys, patients, nurses, doctors, police, and patients' families. His confusion grew as Molly could not detect an open space. He didn't know where in hell he was going to find a parking space while his family could be dying! Suddenly, a pair of red lights lit up, popping from a row of parked vehicles. That was Molly's chance. Once parked, he ran past the mayhem at the entrance, squeezing himself through the crowded lobby to the main desk, somewhat calm enough to announce to the administrator, "I'm Jason Davies looking for Sargent Owens."

Immediately, a quiet voice said, "Mr. Davies, could you please follow me."

As they were walking, as requested, Jason presented his ID to the receptionist, and she pointed to a room to her right and said, "The first room there on the right."

When he entered, he saw three people sitting around a small desk with lots of paperwork on it when suddenly three faces were staring up at him.

"Sargent Owens?" Jason asked, almost whispering, as if he were scared to ask the question.

"Are you Mr. Davies," the Sargent replied as he rose to greet Jason.

"Yes, could you please tell me what's going on and where my wife, daughter, son-in-law, and the baby are?"

"Please sit down here, Mr. Davies," replied what appeared to be a doctor or some medical staff person. "I'm Dr. Berman," extending his hand as Jason began to sit down at the table. At that same moment, Sargent Owens and the other gentleman got up and left the room, and when they did, the silence was noticed. "Please sit down, Mr. Davies." the doctor pointed to the chair. "I am sorry to have to tell you that there was a hideous accident, and your wife, daughter, and son-in-law never had a chance. They were dead on arrival, Mr. Davies." There was dead silence. The doctor was ready for the shock, and it came BIG! He continued, "I know right now there is no such thing as good news, but I can tell you this: it is a blessing, a miracle from above, that the baby

5

is unhurt, probably because his car seat protected him."
Jason's mind could not comprehend. The voice was fading,
and now all he could hear was his heart beating at an
intolerable rate. "Mr. Davies... Mr. Davies, are you all
right?"

Chapter II

They met at the local college coffee shop where all the *master's degrees to be,* gathered. It was a comical, almost planned, slapstick scene. They both had small black coffees and reached for the condiments at the same time, nearly spilling their hot caffeine addictions on each other, both slightly burning their own hands that held their cups, with each gasping an 'oh' simultaneously, then bursting out laughing, not even noticing the continuing *hot* sensation on their hands, as both their shirt sleeves got coffee stained. Their eyes met, and that was it!

Jean (Miller) Davies was the daughter of Simon and Sharon Miller. Simon was a very successful dentist and allowed his daughter to become educated for whatever profession she desired. Jean loved biology. When dissecting a frog in middle school, she was first in line. She had graduated from undergrad school with high honors, was on a scholarship for her master's degree, and was hoping to continue further on to acquire a doctorate degree. She had tons of dates, but no one had struck lightning with her until Jason. Their courtship was energizing and refreshing. They would see each other almost every night throughout their remaining days at grad school, learning to study together in their separate fields and teaching each other while unknowingly securing their compatibility forever. She possessed chestnut-colored hair, sparkling brown eyes, red lipstick on alluring lips, a perfectly clear complexion as though it had been photo touched, and a petite nose. She was five feet, six inches, slim to medium build, with a shapely feminine figure. She wore clothes that were tasteful yet mysterious from a sexual point of view, never exposing too much or too little.

"Establish your career before you go, boy crazy," was what her father used to say, "get your profession established, so you're not forced to marry based on dependency. Find out who you are first," he would continue, "so you know what kind of person you want to share your life with." She remembered those words as she sat down on a sofa with Jason at the coffee shop.

After a few sips of coffee, they listened to each other as their bodies were tingling with excitement, and their smiling faces gave them away. The conversation came so easy. It was engaging, with an abundance of similarities and inconsequential differences, just amazing! Their birthdays were within a year of each other's; their fields were somewhat scientifically connected, their goals of doctorate degrees, attitude toward being educated, respect, patriotism, on and on, almost too good to be true. But there it was. She had never experienced these feelings or thoughts before. She wasn't sure if it was infatuation or the real thing. She heard, saw, and had imagined things about love, but she had yet to experience and learn what love was for herself.

They were healthy eaters, as little as possible of processed foods that contain man-made poisons in them. They loved to jog together, play doubles at the club, do yoga for her, and go to the gym for him. They both believed in natural healing. Mike, their son-in-law, was an up-and-coming chiropractor to whom they paid a visit every week. They were big believers in making adjustments to allow blood to flow continuously unimpeded through their bodies. Blood carries *all* the ingredients for healing. Blood cells, brain cells, the cellular structure of the human body, Jason knew all of it. His main course of study had been how blood cells interacted with the ingestion of processed foods. He wrote his thesis on that subject for his Ph.D. That was the world he owned! He still loved it and accepted that this kind of research takes years of testing and analysis to produce reliable, sensible conclusions, as tiny doses of man-made ingredients build up in the body very, very slowly. He was also well versed in microbiomes, the latest in health nutrition. He strongly agreed with the philosophy that each individual has their own 'food chemistry', which reacts and digests uniquely.

Chapter III

At 1:00 AM, on a cold rainy November morning, Jason Davies was brought forth unto this earth. Jason would be their first and only child. He was a normal-sized baby, but soon after being taken home from the hospital, an unknown virus was making him so ill and sick that he almost died. The doctor who saved his life knew there had been some sort of disease going around the country with similar characteristics. Jason struggled to stay alive, unknowingly fighting for his life for nine months. He never really knew the doctor who saved his life nor the disease that struck him.

Jason's father was born in America, joined the army during the Vietnam War, and became a specialist in CBR (Chemical, Biological, and Radiology). After returning home, he went to college, where he studied vigorously to become a scientist and loved college sports. He was a man with a good heart that loved his son. Jason's father would take him to all the college games, where he, too, would come to love sports. So as they aged together, Jason would learn a great deal about life from his father. His father would say things like, "America is the best country in the world, and you should never waiver in your patriotism. But beware of the power of hungry politicians who run our government. They work for lobbyists for their own financial gains. It's all about greed, payoffs, and plenty of disinformation from the government to hide the truth."

Jason was an exceptionally bright student and played in high school sports. In college, the assigned material came so easily to him. His interest in nutrition began in Jr. High School when a nutritionist came to speak in a science class one day. He was fascinated by what he learned about the body's metabolism and how preventing illnesses and diseases can be accomplished by reading certain signs in the blood and taking counteractions. From that day on, he knew exactly what he wanted to do for the rest of his life. He was excited about learning more about nutrition and was very interested in learning what was needed for healthy growth and what the body rejected as garbage, such as fast foods. He learned that the loss of minerals in the soil leads to shortages in the body, which in turn affects the immune system causing illness and disease and that true healing comes from the body itself, natural healing. He would read, retain the knowledge, experiment with his own body, and record results. By his undergrad college days, he possessed a fit, handsome, 6' tall, muscular body with brown hair and brown eyes. He would graduate high school with an A average and go to college with a fully paid scholarship to study Nutrition and Pathology. His father brought him up believing that The Creator is God and is Nature. But the word 'God' wasn't used by his family because of the word's misuse. So he came to believe in a creator and that each individual is a part of The Creator, and that all religious beliefs have the same basic goals. He grew up learning all of this from his father and all the other important things in life, such as right from wrong, good vs. evil, and respect for other people. He liked girls, but he could never find a good conversationalist that could keep his attention. He was very polite and kind, but the average college girl couldn't keep up with him and probably found him dull whenever he discussed his opinions, mostly about nutrition. He dated girls through high school and college with no true love in his life, and because he was so focused on his career, he didn't notice any particular girl until grad school when Jean bumped into him. He couldn't stop thinking about her after they met at the coffee shop. He knew she would make a beautiful, intelligent, loving wife and that he would do whatever it took to make it happen.

He would end his graduate studies graduating at the top of his class with a Master's Degree in Cytology and Cell Biology in the biotech industry. That's when the US Government became interested in him! They were prepared to offer him a huge two-year grant to complete his Ph.D. in cellular nutrition, specifically, studying the effects of metabolism of artificial nutrients in animals and eventually in human cells. This offer was made only if he agreed to work for the government in the future, and he wouldn't know about his true experimental research project until after he received his Ph.D. He agreed to the grant offer, and after two years, he would be working on a fully-funded project in his field of expertise.

Chapter IV

Jean and Jason's parents had already passed away. Their only child, Susan, married Mike Kellogg, who had grown up in an orphanage with no parents, brothers, or sisters. And now that they were gone, there was no one left except Jason and a week-old baby boy. At first, Jason was noticeably somber, quiet and somewhat withdrawn, not quite listening or attentive to anyone or anything. His mind was blank; his heart was empty. *Am I forty-eight years young,* he thought, *or am I forty-eight years old? What could possibly be next?* he said to himself. He didn't want to think about his future. He didn't eat much that first week. He lost weight. The nights were the worst. The empty bed beside him drew his eyes to tears. The thoughts of Jean passing through his mind like a speeding freight train kept him from sleeping until finally, in the early hours of the dawn, exhaustion overcame his thoughts, the loneliness drifted away and crying ceased into slumber. Waking up to another day was just as bad. Getting out of bed was an effort. *Another day of what?* he thought, and he would roll over and lie there in the quiet. All his morning routine of disciplines of getting up early, taking a morning jog, a shower, dressing for work, making a protein drink for Jean and himself, and his usual stop for coffee were temporally postponed as he mourned. He'd lie in bed at night, not sure about anything anymore.

The second week got a little better. His darkness remained, he needed more time, and soon his thoughts began to center on his own life and being. All sorts of things were popping up in his head. He questioned his own happiness. He was a stickler about word meanings, so ultimately, he discovered that he needed to define happiness and joy because happiness was so elusive now. He again reviewed his past life with Jean and questioned himself about what made him happy and what gave him joy. *What was the difference anyway? Happiness is only temporary; it doesn't come from true love,* he reasoned. *Happiness comes only from a thought. Negative inner thoughts created by one's ego can effectively change happiness to sadness and vice-versa. Joy, on the other hand,* he wanted to believe, *is true love that comes as part of your soul when you come to earth, a natural state of being with inner peace. It's always there. When you don't feel joy, it's covered up by other thoughts such as fear, the opposite of love. One can never really become un-joyed because joy is always there through happiness or sadness.* He summarized that even though there is sadness at the loss of his loved ones, he could at the same time feel joy in the birth of his grandchild. He didn't know why he wanted or needed to determine the difference between those two simple words, but it made him feel alive again, so he was glad he did. And, by the end of the second week, he knew he would always have joy in what he had with Jean, Susan and Mike and the arrival of the new baby.

During the third week away from his job, Jason started to think of his future. He was aware of the void in his life that would come. He was able to hire a woman named Alisa to cook and tend to the house chores, who had been recommended to him by a friend. But no more would he have the love of his life. His eyes would become watery thinking of that. His routines were not yet in play, and he wasn't anywhere near a hundred percent ready to return to work. He stayed in bed much longer than usual, off his health drink, no longer jogging and working out, and by the middle of the week, he was tired, bored, miserable, and now, more empty than ever before. On the last day of the week, he realized that he needed to hit rock bottom before he could recover. The very next day, he woke up feeling a little better. He greeted Alisa with a genuine smile and kept himself occupied so he would be focused on the *now* and not allow negative thoughts to bring him back to the past. He went upstairs to his home office to go through the mail and deal with all the paperwork accumulated during the past weeks. He found himself looking at death certificates and wondering what the wrongful death litigation would be like. He didn't get teary-eyed. He started to get angry but stopped when he thought to let the lawyer handle it, and he put the certificates back in the file folder and sifted through the condolence cards, throwing away all the usual daily trash mail in the recycle bin. Alisa made him a sandwich for lunch, prepared dinner for him late afternoon, and then tended to the baby and herself. All alone again, he wouldn't let himself drift into the negative ego thoughts zone, for he knew what it would do to him, so he kept busy all evening reviewing his analysis of the recent findings of his research.

Chapter V

Zachary (Zack) Blankhardt was a Harvard graduate, being accepted solely based on his wealthy parent's connections, not because of his academic record. He was a very attractive, sexy looking man with extremely good looks. Of course, he was a womanizer; he couldn't help it! It was the way he was brought up. He wasn't book smart, but he was extremely clever, and he could usually get what he wanted. 'Money is king', he would think, always repeating it in his thoughts whenever he needed something. And he would get it. But he wasn't cold. He had a good heart. He just happened to be born with a silver spoon in his mouth. He learned about money from his father, an extremely successful hedge fund trader on Wall Street. His father had told him to go to Harvard and study finance; then, he could work at an investment firm. And so Zack always thought that he would, and that was that. He always had the latest sports car or any new tech gadgets, most anything he wanted. He stood just over six feet tall, medium athletic build with very dark wavy 'Ivy League hair', the kind of hair that doesn't move when he drives with the convertible top down. He was a confident man with a charismatic smile, possessing a smooth masculine bass voice with a slight Boston accent. Zack barely graduated with a BS in Business, and to his father's dismay, he was 'recruited' by his father's brother,

Senator Richard Blankhardt, who was serving as a member of the Armed Forces Services Committee. Zack was hired as part of his uncle's staff and was to serve as a liaison officer, a special aide to General Wilks, a three-star general. The Senator wanted to bring Zachary to Washington to introduce him to the 'who's who and who you know crowd' so that someday Zack could run for office and, who knows, maybe be President! And because of that possibility, the Senator would always try to keep Zack *clean* by never allowing him to *know* anything that could hurt his future chances. After the initial meeting with his uncle and the invitation to join the Senator's staff, Zack daydreamed about the Hollywood stars, politicians, entertainers and glamour girls he might get to meet but didn't exactly explain it to his father that way when he broke the news. He couldn't say, "Why work in the boring investment field when you can mingle with the rich and famous." Instead, he would say something that would disappoint his parents but not horrify them. When the news got broken, his parents *were* disappointed, especially his dad. But in the end, they eventually forgave Zack because his father was very close to his brother. Also, Zack's father noticed a special gleam and excitement in Zack's eyes. Zack would start as a junior staff member to learn the 'ins and outs' of politics and take on special assignments as he grew. "Secrets," his uncle said to him, "it will be your job to find out all our opponents' secrets and expose them to me. You serve and report directly to me or in my absence to General Wilks and no one else! So be alert and unnoticed when you see or hear anything useful, and immediately report back to me. Do you understand?" Zachary nodded.

Chapter VI

Jason Davies was first 'noticed' by the government after obtaining his Master's Degree in Cytology of Animal and Human Digestion. That's when Jason first met Zachary Blankhardt, who was assigned the task of getting Jason to sign a contract with the government. Blankhardt explained that he works for his uncle, US Senator Richard Blankhardt, as a Senior Staff Member and also serves as liaison to General Michael Wilks, Department of Defense, US Army, in their Special Research Grants Department all of which Jason had no idea even existed. In his smooth, confident, convincing 'Boston blue blood demeanor', Zack admitted that the average American was unaware of all the government's top secret projects. Now in his selling mode, Blankhardt told Jason that the contract included a generous financial grant, along with full use of the government's laboratory facility so that he could become accustomed to his surroundings, which would be his lab for the future top secret research project. Jason liked the idea. It made perfect sense, and it appeared to be an efficient use of government resources.

"However," Blankhardt continued, "I must inform you that it is clearly stated in the contract that the US government will own all of your research thesis and your research for the subsequent five-year commitment."

Jason paused for a moment. It was expected; *it's normal government business practice,* he thought, yet it just didn't feel all warm and cozy inside his body, but a few seconds later, Jason said, "I understand."

In addition, Jason was told by Blankhardt, "By contract, you specifically agree to work on the five-year research project alone, with assistants, of course, but they will only perform menial research tasks. It will be you, and only you, who will be conducting laboratory test procedures, analysis and reporting to higher authorities. Not even your wife can know the exact purpose or procedures of the project… no one!" Zack explained. "The research project you will be working on is so top secret that even I… don't know what it's about! And it's not being revealed to you until after you receive your PhD. If and when the time comes, Jason, I will be your liaison, and your *only* liaison, between you and the people responsible for the project, that is, Senator Blankhardt and General Wilks. Eventually," he went on, "you will meet with them, and that's when they will then explain the project's purpose and mission. There is one thing I can tell you, Jason, and that is, I was specifically instructed to inform you, from the people I mentioned I work for, if successful, this research project could save lives, be a huge benefit to America and is valuable, noble and creditable service to your government and country. At this stage, that's all I can tell you. I'm sorry if I've left you with a lot of unanswered questions." Jason nodded and shrugged his shoulders. They smiled at each other, and as they were shaking hands, Zack handed Jason his business card and said, "Take a little time and when ready, contact me as soon as you make a decision."

Chapter VII

"I know there must be a good reason why someone would trade seven good years of their life working for the government with no future! It's money! And plenty of it! I have no idea where the money to pay my salary will come from. I assume it will be coming from somewhere in the Defense Department," he explained to Jean. "And the security measures are extreme; it's top secret. That what's this guy...some government liaison agent named Zack Blank...something" as he took Zack's card from his pocket and peered at it. "Yes, that's it, Zachary Blankhardt. He works for his uncle, Senator Richard Blankhardt, some big shot who is a member of the Armed Forces Services Committee. Said he was a senior staff member but also serves as a liaison between his uncle and some General in the Defense Department. He told me that the project was so top secret that even he knew nothing about it, and that I won't be told about it until after I receive my PhD. By contract," he went on, "I'm not even supposed to tell you, my soon to be wife, such secrets!" he quietly whispered. There was a pause of silence, and in that moment, Jason recalled his father's words about political greed, *trusting* the people who run the country and how governments can so easily distort the truth. *The FBI must have already investigated him and Jean, too,* he thought. He went on,

24

"Blankhardt told me that the people behind the two-year thesis grant and the five-year research project wanted me to know that if this project is successful, it will save lives, be beneficial to the whole free world, and I will be performing valuable and honorable service to my country."

"Was there anyone else chosen for this project?" Jean inquired.

"No one else," he said, "I am supposed to conduct this research independently, except I can hire some graduate students, as assistants, to do some low-level research, probably inconsequential to the project. The test procedures, analysis and reports to superiors are to be exclusively done by me and only me. I really won't know anything more until the project is revealed. They said that one reason they can pay me an incredibly higher salary and benefits than I could get from any other company or institution in my specialty is because of hiring only one main researcher for the project. Anyway, it's coming at a great time in our lives," said Jason, with Jean agreeing.

They discussed their marriage plans and children, and since Jean would be finishing her PhD the same time as Jason, they would find an apartment to get her moved into the city where Jason's new lab would be located. With Jason's salary, Jean could find a position without the stress of urgency. They talked further.

"Jean, I know you remember what we said about trust before we got engaged," he said.

"Yes, I do, Jason," she replied. "That whatever one of us knows, both of us know."

"There will never be an exception to that agreed promise from me, Jean," Jason responded, "even though I may breach my contract with the government, YOU will always know everything. You are my everlasting love and confidante. Nothing or no one will ever come before you," he exclaimed.

After discussing the fact that it was only a five-year contract, they finally decided that Jason would sign. Making the decision gave them comfort and peace. Doing work in his field of expertise brought excitement to Jason; he was a happy camper. Everything seemed to fit perfectly!

While Zack was finishing his two-year training period in the political field as a grunt, Jason completed his two-year government PhD grant in cellular nutrition. At their second meeting to sign the contract, they spoke to each other casually after the more serious business was concluded. As they conversed further, Jason found out that even though Zachary was just a few years older, Zack was also a newcomer to the US government, working as an aide to General Wilks, the officer in charge of Jason's research project. They both seemed comfortable with each other, not knowing they were 'exact opposites' in many aspects of their lives. In the years that followed, they became 'working friends'. Zack would make occasional unannounced visits to Jason's lab but had no knowledge or interest whatsoever in medical research, science, or anything else connected to the project. He was never informed nor learned the missions or any detail of all the special projects he was assigned and didn't care because all he wanted to learn was how inside politics *really* worked. Jason, on the other hand, was focused on his PhD work, The Effects of Artificial Ingredients Consumed in Processed Foods. *Who knows what the next research title will be,* he thought.

Chapter VIII

They were married now, and lo and behold; Jean got pregnant shortly after their wedding. She had already accepted a position with NDCC (National Disease Control Center). This private company mirrored the government's CDC but took on tougher tasks dealing with the most toxic agents. She requested a postponement of her employment until after the baby arrived, which was approved. Soon, baby Susan was born, and what a joy for them! Jean was excited to set up the baby's room for a girl and loved the motherhood of breastfeeding her baby. Jason played the role of father as much as he could with a newborn, picking her up in his arms and speaking softly, "I love you," and watching her play with her mobile while making funny faces to make her laugh at him. The new baby's grandparents were alive then, and on the weekends, they would visit their parents' houses so they could enjoy their granddaughter. Jason and Jean ensured that the food being fed to her was nutritious, clean, and satiating. Children's habits are formed at a very early stage in their life, and Jason and Jean were well aware of that fact. They believed that developing taste buds was very important, and avoiding sugar overload helped to curb future *cravings* while growing up. Good nutrition would always be invoked in their family as a long-standing commitment. After all, don't parents have an obligation to teach and practice good health habits to their children?

While Jean was caring for her new baby Susan, Jason spent most of his life in the laboratory making astonishing discoveries about processing methods of food products in the food manufacturing industry. He learned that some food processors infuse artificial ingredients into their foods to enhance taste, increase water weight, make the product's appearance more 'salable', and extend shelf life with preservatives using long, newly created unpronounceable words on their labels. He found one company that added ingredients to give the eater a craving for more. He believed that processed sugar addiction was real, and the country's sugar product consumption was increasing yearly. He recalled previous research studies that he had read, specifically remembering a study he had seen about laboratory mice being induced to become addicted to sugar and cocaine. When allowed to consume one or the other, they chose sugar over cocaine. And then another recent study he read concluded sugar was 80 times more addictive than cocaine! "Huh," he said while laughing, "sugar is more addictive than cocaine. What a disservice to the human body," he thought. *"Anything* in excess to the body, as adaptable as it has proven to be, overpowers its ability to function properly, and unintended consequences lead to chronic maladies."

Previously in his education, he had read many studies and documents, but now it was more concentrated on manufactured foods. Reading so many documents with so many different results and opinions left him thoroughly confused at times, and over time he began to understand that the most important part of any research study was not necessarily the subject of the report but who performed the analysis, who sponsored the research and why was it done. As he grew up, his research studies left him with trust issues. It was difficult for him to separate black from white because there were studies that contradicted each other. It was impossible to get a definitive answer. And with food, it was even more difficult. If someone was unknowingly ingesting minute doses of toxic, untested chemicals over a long period of time, it is possible that eventually, the body could become 'poisoned' without the person ever knowing it. Symptoms may not appear most times until it's too late to counter them and instead become cancerous and must be dealt with. He would read a medical research paper and then stop to think about it before drawing any conclusions. Over his lifetime, he probably read thousands of pages of percentages. He learned that when some companies tested a new product or re-made an old one, the final numbers given to the public were only used when it benefited the company, not necessarily the consumer. Its purpose was to increase customer confidence to sell more product(s). Even then, the data displayed by the company in its advertising could easily be misleading. For example, a study may conclude that of the remaining 48% of 860 people who experienced no symptoms over one year, there were the remaining 52% who suffered symptoms, but there were 34% who experienced more symptoms over six months than the remaining 66%, who experienced fewer symptoms, etc., etc., and therefore 24% of the remaining people benefited. "What? Everything gets distorted in the percentages," he would say out loud to himself: "Manipulated by the company who paid for the research, using the numbers to make it look better than it may be? And why would a company ever publish or make public an unfavorable study? Where's the money in that? His research only reinforced his belief that with so many different ways to process food and so many different artificial chemicals being used, it is impossible for government agencies to test products for long-term effects properly and thus only proves how much is NOT known. That's what he had to deal with! The pervasive use of artificially made products was firmly entrenched in this country. "Side effects listed on drugs, a warning on cigarettes. Will it be on a box of cereal someday, a laundry list of possible side effects?" he thought. The fact of the matter is that some food manufacturers don't know the long-term effects of their artificial ingredients. His frustration was tempered by the fact that earlier in his life, he had known these things for a long time and made conscious choices in his water, food, and physical activities to maintain his good healthy habits.

He didn't discover much about the different names, combinations, or amounts of ingredients the manufacturers listed on their products. There were thousands. It was overwhelming, and for what purpose? A company, feeling pressure from a lack of supply or cost increase in an ingredient, may decide to change to a cheaper brand. It happens all the time. The final product will change depending on how much is used or how dominant that ingredient is in the product. The variables now change. Where did the ingredient come from? Who grew it? What kind of fertilizer was used? Did it grow in soil devoid of its minerals? Who, when, and how was it processed? If you take just a loaf of bread and change its flour, the new flour will react differently with all the other ingredients, changing the product's variables significantly. However, if you change the type of salt in a bread recipe, the change in the variables may not be noticeably different. Now take the variables of the human body and what you've got are more variables, making everything even more difficult. Does a healthy person digest differently than an unhealthy one? Does the time of day matter when you ingest the ingredients? It can go on endlessly. That's just one reason one must be aware of what foods to choose. So why did the government want him?

They know all these things. Superficially, the study is about the effects of ingesting artificially made ingredients, but according to a lot of research papers, the effects are already known. Previously, Jason's education was mostly concerned about the effects of ingesting modified foods and foods with added substances. What he didn't know was that his research would have nothing to do with helping people eat healthier but that it would be about how toxic invaders get into the body's cells and what happens thereafter. That's the road the research project would be on.

During his two-year study, Jason recorded everything precisely, and now his two-year grant was coming to an end. He had a lot of references, data, and conclusions in his final synopsis but knew nothing that would change anyone's eating habits, let alone change the world. He mainly studied the cellular structure and reactions to digesting toxins of artificial ingredients fed to animals. He had tested many different ingredients, varying the doses over various times. Two years was certainly not a long enough time to see substantial reactions, but in some cases, some test animals died, and when they did, he would perform an autopsy to learn more tolerance levels of the substances being used. It wasn't anything that could be published, not that he could publish anything because of his contract. However, he still didn't understand why the government, especially the army, cared about how toxins were diffused within the cells or how the cells reacted to the toxins. Was the army concerned about preservatives in their rations? Did the government know something that they labeled top secret and then withhold that information from the public so it could be corrected slowly without being detected so as not cause a national panic? Everything was being kept under wraps, *secrets*. He was very anxious to meet with his Grantors now and know what his next five-year research project would entail.

Chapter IX

"What?" Jason said. "You can't be serious! You want me to create something like a super... man?"

"Well...almost," replied the Senator.

"Almost?" declared Jason. Three men were sitting in the Senator's soundproof office, two, who appeared to look insane at that moment, and one dumbfounded with his mouth still open, looking at the insane men with his eyes wide open and a quizzical look on his face. General Wilks spoke first.

"If we told you when you were first offered the contract, we were afraid of this precise reaction. Let me explain and see if I can bring it into perspective. Robots are the first step in using machines to perform the tasks of infantrymen. It's called *Ro-boots on the ground*. Remote-controlled robots can't 'feel' the enemy or the situation and cannot make immediate field decisions that our special forces and seals require. They're vulnerable to hand grenades, artillery, etc. There are times when human senses are necessary, and to date, that's what's missing in machines. If a machine is wounded, or should I say, out of action, it's useless. Even one well-placed round could bring it down. We need to make some humans with impenetrable skin to serve on our special forces and seal teams. We know other countries are trying to accomplish the same thing. I know it sounds utterly fantastic, science fiction stuff, but we feel we would be remiss if we didn't attempt it." "Don't we already give Kevlar vests to them?" Jason asked.

"Of course," replied the General, "but you know as well as I do that they're heavy, have only limited coverage to stop a propellant, and are usually not worn all the time because the men sweat heavily in the warmer climates," the General went on. "We need to create a shield inside the human body."

"So as I understand you, General Wilks," Jason said, "You think a human can grow a kind of hard-like shell like a turtle?"

"Not like a turtle Dr. Davies, but hidden within the skin, undetected, so that the enemy can't pick them apart from an ordinary robotic soldier," replied the General.

There was a noticeable pause.

"I realize, sir, that tremendous strides have been made in the field of human DNA and technical advances in cell research and body implants, but has anyone thought about the feasibility and the amount of time this kind of experiment could take?" questioned Jason.

"Yes, Jason," answered the Senator, "and the longer we wait, the more time we lose. We've got to start now to stay ahead of anyone else, especially while the finances are available to do this project. The General and I have secured enough funds to start and keep this top-secret project going for the next five years, and if we can show some progress over that time, we're certain we can persuade the committee to finance at least an additional five, and maybe ten years. You have been chosen for this project because you are the best in your field, and we believe you can do it alone. That saves us money, money we can use to pay you far more than you could make anywhere else. Call it a generous incentive Jason, because if anyone can do it, our bet's with you."

There was dead silence.

Part Two: The Research Project

Chapter X

Buried side by side, the funeral for Jean, Susan, and Mike was devastating for Jason. There were no more tears left. The sorrow was unbearable. The thought of bringing up the baby brought fear to him. The baby had been home for almost a week, and luckily Alisa agreed to move into the house to take care of the infant while Jason was trying to understand the purpose of his life. He pleaded with himself to find out why. Was it the unnatural project he had worked on, trying to create a human monster? Could that be it? Was he being punished for trying to alter the human body? Didn't other discoveries go against the natural human body, like titanium implants, pacemakers, and contact lenses? That question would taunt him.

From the very beginning and over the length of the research, Jason and Jean always had lasting concerns. But before Jason signed the contract, they *had* thought things through. And, they had realized that, as ridiculous as it seemed, if the project was successful, only the Grantors would be holding all the research documents, and with those *secrets*, why would they need him anymore? To them, as well as to the government, he was expendable. Even though it might take many years to create a human skin of armor, the Senator and the General could use this creation for their own selfish benefit, or even worse, sell the information to someone else! It wasn't just hearing his father's words in his head, over and over again, about trusting people in government. It was the way his research reports were being presented to the committee and the subsequent articles in newspapers, magazines, and other periodicals he read about the Senator's views on the use of armed forces and opinions on many other issues. He wasn't sure whether the Senator was doing these things for the country's good, for himself, or both, so Jason would always proceed "with caution." From the very beginning, *everything* Jason learned was conveyed and discussed with Jean. Again, after thinking through his contract commitment with the government concerning the ownership of the research documents and the high possibility of the program being canceled after five years or at any time for that matter, Jason and Jean decided they were going to keep a separate "pin-head" file (a replacement of the old "flash-drive") that *only* he and Jean would know about. And since he knew he could never remove, or even attempt to remove, anything from his high-security, top-secret laboratory, he would use his photographic memory to memorize his daily research activities and accomplishments, go directly home and then enter his memorized data onto his pin-head. This way, if he was ever asked the question: "Have you ever removed anything from your research lab?" he could answer the question definitively as "No." He actually felt good about that decision because, as weird as it sounds, he felt he could be the counterbalance to any unintended consequences as a result of success. No one else would be monitoring anything about this project, and he felt insecure in that respect. What *if* their intentions were misguided?

His whole life, five days a week, was consumed with his research. Only on the weekends did Jason live a normal family life, taking Jean and young Susan to his college sports events, skiing, or to the beach. Otherwise, his thoughts were always consumed with the project. As sure as the sun rises, Jason would return home and immediately load that day's memorization on the pin-head, relax with Jean in the sunroom, share anything new and listen to the events of her day. Most of Jason's project life was pretty much a normal routine. The lab security was of the highest level. He would pass through the security circle, the screen carefully viewed by an alert security officer, and then he would place his index finger on the fingerprint identification box, insert his federal identification card and open the steel laboratory door. Soon, the security personnel recognized the Dr. and quickly became friends. It would be security who would be responsible for accounting for all the test animals used for the project. Eventually, when the animals were brought into the lab, they were each tagged with a number with all information listed on the tag. Likewise, any animals that had to be removed from the premises had to be accounted for along with the facts of the disposal. At the beginning of gathering information and analysis, which took years, the laboratory section with the animal cages stayed dormant. Later, when the lab experiments began, the days became more regimented. Among many other characteristics, research work requires methodical dedication, calm repetition, meticulous documentation, and, oh, of course, patience. This would be monotonous work to most people, but not to Dr. Jason Davies.

Early morning test evaluations from the previous day's substance ingestion were the first order of business. Measuring day-to-day progress with his lab test animals was a tedious task. The late mornings and afternoons after lunch were used to make new concoctions of substances made from exotic herbs along with other various secret materials and formulas designed by a super-computer to be catalysts to help metabolize the concocted minutia powders, one of which was an extremely secret alloy made of pulverized stainless steel and titanium, thought to be the key to preventing human injury. The amounts were such a minutia they could be seen only under a super-microscope, so powerful and new that only the government possessed it. The later afternoon was used to feed those computer formulas to the lab animals. When that was accomplished, he would enter all the new information into the computer, go through the security check on his way out and start all over again the next day. In the evenings, some of the graduate students Jason hired would come into the lab and clean and care for the animals, while others were allowed to do limited tests on the animals, specially designed by Jason to give no clue as to what his real purpose was. On the weekends, the students were allowed to feed the animals their already computerized prepared food amounts in an individual labeled container for each weekend day. He would use many different animals to test, many times using the same formula on two or more of the same species and different animals. If one subject died and the other(s) didn't, the amount of substance might be held to the same amount or reduced, and in that way, a tolerance level might be determined. As expected, it was a slow trial and error process. This went on day after day for years until one day; he could actually see an unusual growth beginning within the animal's cells that made his face light up. That discovery gave Jason a sense of hope that maybe this crazy idea could work. He went home, entered the prized information into his file, and anxiously described his new findings to Jean.

Jason was directed to submit semi-annual reports to General Wilks, who would then review the reports and submit his comments to the Senator, who in turn would advise the sub-committee. Zack Blankhardt was directed to make several visits to the lab per month to *oversee* the project and to assist Dr. Davies in any of his needs and requests. From the start, Jason was given a super-computer, an upgrade over the older 'Watson', to feed all his information into. That was his starting point. He called the computer *Genie*, partly because it sounded like his wife's name and mostly because he believed that's what it would take to accomplish this project, a genie in a bottle! After all the mountains of information were entered, which took months, he began to ask Genie questions. The purpose was to begin to narrow down the number of substances and their combinations that could be possibilities. That alone could take a long time without ever performing one laboratory test. In the early years, only detailed technical facts and computer data were given in the reports to his superiors because Dr. Davies didn't know what to say. The reports revealed no real progress being made during those years, and the Senator and General could not understand all the technical parts, so basically, the reports conveyed that nothing had been discovered…yet. The reports, however, could not possibly have been submitted to the committee and had to be re-written. Project funds had to be acquired from a *positive* point of view.

Up to now, Dr. Jason Davies led a scholar's life in a somewhat sheltered world. All his friends had been highly educated and mostly worked in the Bio-Tech industry. Before accepting the army's research contract, Jason could talk to his friends, colleagues, and fellow alumni about his work in nutrition and any topic with mutual respect and understanding. He was always comfortable and kind in his social surroundings, being a patient listener rather than an 'interrupter' and always paused to think through a question when asked to respond. He knew or learned those things early in life when he discovered 'stress'. In the many studies he had read, patients would usually identify their illness with some stress going on in their life, and he could not, not pay attention to it. He concluded that stress plays a common leading role in sickness by constricting the blood flow and halting normal body operations, producing elevated fear chemicals, and creating tension. When he started noticing what stress did, he became aware of the moment he began to physically 'feel' the change in his chemistry. The first few times felt like an electrical shock going through him in a millisecond, restricting his blood vessels and causing him to become tense. As time passed, his 'awareness' taught him to listen and trust his body's communication. That's how he came to know that awareness can create change. He discovered that tension invites stress, but *once recognized*, that is, once he understood that stress was self-imposed on the way he reacted to a situation and not the situation itself, the stress disappeared because his focus changed from the situation to the 'awareness' of the chemical reaction inside his body (the communication), which meant, paying attention to the chemical change in his body notified him stress was swiftly approaching. As author Eckhart Tolle explains in one of his books read by Jason: "It's never the situation that causes stress, but the negative thoughts around it." It was almost as if Dr. Jason Davies was born a wise man, and the Creator had gifted him the 'talent' of wisdom and understanding that one's body does communicate.

In his first report, after six months on the job, he wrote: "Presently entering pertinent information into the computer, and will continue to do so until complete. Expect probability list within the next 12-18 months." Neither more information nor details were necessary, and nothing further was required or expected. Without sounding like he was complaining, he wanted to show the complexity of deciding what data, such as elements that may help metabolize artificial substances, growth hormones, etc., needed to be entered into the super-computer because of the infinite possibilities of multiple combinations of selected substances. Without Genie's help, it would have taken thousands, maybe millions of years, and people to accomplish what Genie could do. Jason knew that when Genie started producing some potential solutions, actual testing could begin. The following two years of his reports were similar to the first, short and to the point, as it took that long before testing would begin.

Just past the fourth year, the first reason to cheer happened. That was when Dr. Davies discovered the unusual chain inside newly grown cells of chimpanzees. A wide variety of animals had ingested the same formula, but the new cells under his super-microscope were only visible in chimpanzees. He was excited and pleased with this discovery because of the close similarities between a chimpanzee's and a human's DNA. He felt he now had at least a path to follow with this particular formula, something he could follow where he could adjust the amounts of ingredients. He was excited but needed to remain low-key before bringing the news to Jean. For the last year remaining on his contract, Jason would track that formula, losing some animals while adjusting to the remaining living animals to determine limits. Progress at last! The Grantors would be pleased, and as planned, Senator Blankhardt, still the leading senior senator on the committee, secured an additional five years of funding for the project, six months before it ended. Once again, it would be Zack Blankhardt who would be used to get Dr. Davies's signature on the new, more lucrative contract. It worked again!

Over those next five years, with the help of Jason's huge increase in salary, savings, and small investments, his wealth grew to a size where he could now become a significant investor in the Biotech and DNA industries, something he always kept up with through his science colleagues. And when some of the companies he invested in sold stock to the public on an Initial Public Offering, he made a killing. His net worth grew beyond his wildest dreams. However, with the discovery of the new cells, the project work became much more interesting to him. The desire to be a millionaire investor and leave his work never crossed his mind. As he continued his advances, he mostly watched the chimpanzees as they were consistently growing those new types of cells. He recorded their physical actions, always checked their vitals, and looked for any change. What was appearing in their cells under a special super-microscope, he didn't exactly know, but his gut feeling told him to stay the course, remain in hot pursuit.

Chapter XI

Those five years proved to be fruitful. Most of the other species of animals died, but not the chimpanzees, they all survived. Jason assumed that since the amount of formula given was not lethal to them, he would now take a select number of them and change the amounts of certain substances, leaving a few with no change whatsoever in their formula and even leaving fewer with no formula. He performed special tests to determine what the new breed of cells had done to the animals' health and natural reactions and could find no distinct changes over the six years since the first discovery. So, nearing the conclusion of his second contract, he could only report further growth of these new cells, only seen with his highly sensitive instruments and equipment. His final report after ten years on the project was that he believed something new was happening, but as yet, didn't know, and it might be detectable with more time. So he informed his Grantors, who were still in place near the end of his contract, that further study was necessary, and of course, he knew more funds would have to be approved. It was time again, for the third time to utilize the services of Zack, now a young politician still under the Senator's thumb, who became a state legislator. His uncle, Senator Richard Blankhardt, who had his election race coming up in two years, succeeded in getting the funds for what he thought would be the final contract of this Project. This year was a presidential election, and a change in his party's strength would most definitely affect his future political life.

The third contract held the same salary but offered a huge bonus for succeeding in the mission of producing the formula that could create a super-soldier. Again it was seriously talked about between husband and wife. Jean had been back working as soon as her daughter was old enough and was very happy in her job. Jason wanted to see his Project to the end as long as he could, so the new contract was signed. The Project would continue. However, in the next two years, only one male chimpanzee was given the formula and survived. Jason then decided to keep only one female chimpanzee, given nothing but normal food. He would keep them separated until the right moment. So, finally, after twelve years of research, only two experimental animals were left, a female chimpanzee that was given nutritious food with no formula and a male chimpanzee receiving the formula producing increased amounts of this new type of cell but still no signs of change to the permeability of his skin. In the November election, Senator Richard Blankhardt lost in his battle for re-election and retired. Coinciding with that event, General Wilks quickly submitted his request for retirement and was approved. Jason's research would go on with no more reports required because the Grantors were gone, and Zack was to be coached by his uncle to run for his seat in the next election. No one else on the Armed Services Committee was interested, had paid much attention to, or even cared about the project. The Project was already financed for the next three years and was simply overlooked. In his final report to his Grantors, Dr. Davies would explain the progress made, but again more time would be needed to draw any conclusions.

In the thirteenth year of the project, something strange happened. The formula fed male chimpanzee which started growing noticeably larger and, when tested, began to show signs of increased strength. Its skin became tougher and would heal instantly from a cut or bruise, but it did not yet know if it was impermeable, as was the mission's main purpose. But now, Jason could follow the growing cell structures, the increase in strength and size, and the healing power of the blood measured between the two remaining chimpanzees. Dr. Jason Davies's research was becoming exciting, and instead of being discouraged by the loss of his supporters, he became even more intent on following through. He now had a formula that made him feel excited and scared simultaneously. From this time forward, he would continue to feed the male chimpanzee the formula and measure the growth in size and strength. He wanted to know if the cell structures would differ over time. They most certainly did! Over the last two years of his employment, he discovered that feeding the formula to the male increased its cells, strength, and healing power, while the female, who ate nutritious food without the formula, remained status quo, with no signs of loss or gain in the studied attributes.

Very interesting!

A few months before the day ended his contract, Jason had an idea he wanted to discuss with Jean. He wanted to form his own one-man research company and continue the work he had started.

"By giving more time to this experiment. I've been working on it for the last thirteen years of my life. There could be important discoveries hidden in time. Why throw it all away?" he said to Jean. "We've got so much money; both of us could retire and still live very comfortably for the rest of our lives." They both needed to think about it overnight, and by the next evening, they had made a plan. He had to see it through on his own, and he was very pleased Jean agreed. To get what he needed, he would have to play the game and use the political, "Who you know?" because the, "What you know?" to a government, especially to a hired security company, "means nothing." This meant that the only person in the world that could help him right now was Zack Blankhardt.

How ironic! They had remained friends over the years, and now Jason needed a favor from a friend. It was no secret that he would use his new assets for future research, which he intended to do on his own, and having Zack know that in the fifteen years they had known each other. Jason had always kept his word, never leaking anything to the media, never suspected or investigated by anyone, Jason thought Zack would feel safe in allowing the purchase. He knew that every favor from a politician came with some payback. He just didn't know when, where or how it would be repaid, but he trusted his and his wife's judgment and decision, so he submitted a special and unusual request to Zack. "Is there a possibility of purchasing certain items from the government that was located in the laboratory, among which included two surviving chimpanzees?" he sent to Zack. He waited. On the last day of his contract commitment, when the security company confiscated everything, he was pleasantly surprised that his request was approved. The security company recorded the transaction and sent it to Zack's office along with a signed document from Dr. Jason Davies stating he would never disclose his past project to anyone.

Over the next five years, the most important information concerning the formula fed chimpanzee, now named Hercules, was the increase of new chain cells, strength, and energy. As for the female chimpanzee, Venus never received the secret formula again. Dr. Davies had plans for her use in the future. He continued closely monitoring the formula's effects or non-effects on Hercules, who remained and appeared healthy with no known side effects. As time went on, the differences became even more apparent. He was pleased with the progress and ready to look at the next step until that horrible day that took the lives of his family. At that point, if everything went to hell, he didn't care!

Part Three: The Plan Creation

Chapter XII

The baby was brought home while Jason mourned, he had sense enough to explain to Alisa that the infant would get a healthier start if breastfed. Since that was not available, it was extremely important to know exactly what and when to feed his new grandson. *Never* anything with processed sugar! He sat down at his computer and produced a 28-day feeding program with directions. Nutritious ingredients were already mixed within baby food jars. It was a good start and would be continuously adjusted as the boy grew. The baby and Alisa were now living in the guest room, leaving silence in the rest of the house. Having this first step off his mind and now living in the quiet, his mind drifted everywhere, all day long.

"Why?" asked Jason, looking up, imagining someone was there. "Was it ordained? Is there some purpose in going through so much pain? I've lost all that I loved, and I am just left with a baby, for what reason?" He was angry! He knew exactly how survivors had felt after losing their family in the war, or for that matter, any event when a family is lost. It would take days before anything positive came out of him. Jason and Jean had practiced spirituality as their faith. The emerging despair prevented him from accepting past events and seeing, believing in, or embracing the future. His mind was feeding him all negative thoughts, creating anger and despair. He couldn't think straight, sleep, or work. He kept trying to reason with himself and sort things out. He tried to find a purpose for his life now that he alone was responsible for the infant's welfare. His thoughts flooded his mind.

From out of the ashes, does a Phoenix always arise? Was he being summoned to do something special?

He wanted to go back to view the path his life had taken. *Were the past life's events coincidences or fate?*

He started seeing a thread connecting important events in his life.

Why am I even thinking this way? It's crazy!

Why are these images coming into my head? Was all my life leading to this moment?

He stopped, dead in his tracks.

"IMPOSSIBLE!!" he blurted out loud. "Feed the formula to my... my own grandson?" Suddenly, he could hear Zack's voice conveying his Grantors' first message to him.

If successful, it will save lives, be a benefit to America, and you would be performing honorable, noble, and valuable service to your country.

He thought of Jean and wanted to speak to her. Oh, how he missed her! He needed her counsel, so he said softly, "Jean, I have in my hands the opportunity of making a human being who would possess great strength and great healing power, our grandchild," *Hercules*. "I know it's crazy, but why am I even thinking I have the right to do such a thing to a human being, to my flesh and blood? What?" he pleaded. "What gives me the right to think that way?" Daily, he would meditate, calm himself in the quiet surroundings, and listen for an answer. It crossed his mind that he, as the *'mad scientist,'* had brought forth his perverted thoughts to be examined, and now the agony over the decision would begin. Being on the fence, that is, the time expended to make the decision can be brutal, judging its morality, its justification, its commitment, its high risk of failure with unimaginable consequences. Its secrecy, its execution, its cost, its worth, its madness, and oh yes, its purpose, yes…its purpose? The formula had only been tested on an animal, *never* human beings!

Who or what put this idea into his head anyway? Even if nature allowed it to be successful, what the hell was he supposed to do with a human Hercules?

Then one night, somewhere from a dream filled sleep, his upper body suddenly popped up to a sitting position like a jack-in-the-box. It was 3:20 in the morning. After feeling the sweat on his body and wiping his eyes to see the time, Jason put his hands over his face attempting to remember Jean's words in his dream. What happened in that dream that made him jump awake? He was thinking…thinking. There was no way he could go back to sleep. He had to stay awake now to understand the meaning of Jean's words to him. Both did not believe in a list of religious rules and regimentation; rather, they were highly spiritual and had learned about universal vibrations, channeling reincarnation, and crossover stories. Both strongly believed in the metaphysical vibration connection and that if the mind and body can focus on listening the answer is always there, maybe hidden in a dream, a daydream, or meditation, nevertheless, always there. He went into the kitchen with the night lights on, put on the teapot of water to boil, and sat down at the kitchen table. Once again closing his eyes with his head resting in his hands. "Football game?" flashed in his thoughts. "I'm at a football game with Jean, Zack, Senator Blankhardt, and General Wilks?" The next thing that popped into his mind, everyone was standing in the stadium when Jean leaned over his shoulder, whispering in his ear, "You know Jason, anything is possible if it's done in true LOVE." Then he saw himself looking down on the football field only to see that all the players were chimpanzees! He couldn't remember anything after that. He went back to his thoughts to see if he could get back to learn anything else, but simultaneously, the tea kettle spout exhaled a stream of steam, creating a loud whistle that startled him. He turned off the kettle, pulled out his cup that said 'Greatest Husband Ever,' put it in the tea bag, poured the steaming water in, and brought it to the table.

Turning around from the table, he opened the drawer to the kitchen desk, pulled out a pen and pad, and wrote, 'Anything is possible if it's done in true LOVE.' He sat at the table staring at the words, sipping his cup of tea, almost timelessly, until finally, he felt his eyes start to close.

Chapter XIII

He woke up the following morning amazingly refreshed, kissed the baby as he did every morning, and gave Alisa a hearty 'Good Morning' along with instructions for the day. She noticed the change in him, more life and more vigor. He looked sharper and more in control of himself. She smiled back with the same greeting. He returned to his old routine and went off to jog somewhere quiet. He felt free. He felt exhilarated by the fact that he had recaptured her words, her message. Even though the dream might be a riddle to be unraveled, he was excited to have what he considered an answer. He would jog today with a mission to find out what this all meant. But, instead of thinking about the dream, his thoughts went to his grandson. Almost four weeks old with no parents, brothers, sisters, cousins, grandmothers, and only one grandfather. Stephen Kellogg, an infant whose life had been spared in a head-on collision with a drunken truck driver, had survived. That alone had to be considered a miracle! Was he saved for some special reason, to do something great? He wanted to tie together the dream he had last night with that miracle and the amazing coincidence that after many years of research with the results of having a healthy, energized chimpanzee, he was already considering human testing anyway.

After all, weren't humans already breathing, drinking, and ingesting poisons? Did it matter if it wasn't intentional? And don't chimpanzees have 94% of the same DNA as humans?

After he finished his jog and before he showered, he sat down at the kitchen table, picked up the pad, and read Jean's words again. That night, it happened in bed again. At about the same time as the previous night, he woke up suddenly, raising the top half of his body in a quick movement, settling perpendicular to the bed. Listening, this time, he would immediately recall his dream. He sat there still in a dizzy, dreamy state when suddenly a vision showed that he was flying through clouds on a big bird... *bird?* He could only see hazy shadows through the clouds. *Wait...who is that?* He saw what he thought was the outline of a man, then more outlines of what appeared to be two women, one with an infant in her arms. Everything was gray and cloudy with no color. He tried to see their faces but to no avail. It was too fuzzy. When those images left, other images were flying by his vision at great speed when all of a sudden, a framed black and white picture of George Washington stopped in front of his face and said, "All the universe must be in balance," then faded away when suddenly appeared a vision of the Statue of Liberty. And that disappeared without a sound as fast as it came. Off in the far distance, in the corner of his eye, his attention was drawn to a tiny speck of red approaching him through a dense fog. It was the first color to appear in the clouds. As it came closer and closer to him, he started seeing redder, then blue, and last, white. *What appeared to be.... a... a flag, the American flag... on a flag pole?*

As the image flashed by him, he could have sworn he saw the iconic Marine photo of the flag being raised on Iwo Jima. When the image disappeared, he looked down at his feet. He saw that they were covered with a sea of footballs, as far as he could see, when suddenly, the huge bird he had been traveling on flew over him, and in a blink of an eye, exposed itself just enough so that Jason could recognize it... the mythical Phoenix Bird! That's when he abruptly woke up. He went to the kitchen again as he had done the previous night, making tea, but this time he sat down at the table and started writing down his visions. He started to piece the puzzle together step by step when suddenly he jumped to his feet, swung both arms up to the sky like a referee signaling a 'Touchdown', and yelled, "I got it! I understand. Thank you, Jean."

Now he felt he had a purpose in his life with the energy and excitement of a younger man. He would create a Plan. Stephen H Kellogg, the 'H' (Hercules) now added to his name at this very moment by Jason. It was the beginning of a mythical journey!

Chapter XIV

The child was the focus now. *Very much the focus!* The agony of what he had gone through to make such a decision was bewildering, but at least it was over. The thoughts surrounding the decision created by the mind, the Ego, is where the human agony lies. Once a decision is made, thoughts concerning the decision are no longer required, and without the thoughts, thank goodness. The agony dies. He had given himself a two month deadline, two months of agony. The memory would live with him forever. Right after the decision, he started organizing his mind. Jason had to think of a plan to accomplish what he set out to do.

First and foremost, if all went well with the formula, his Grandson would gain strength and agility. Second, provide an intense education tempered with common sense (if it can be taught!), respect for all life, healthy eating and personal health routines, proper social manners, and a positive attitude toward life. For that, he needed a unique nanny, a highly educated young woman in nutrition, sports, and body conditioning, able to live on the premises long-term to educate the boy as he grows up. He wanted someone who could speak many languages fluently and possess the gift of a teacher. Not an easy task. So Jason planned to give this search plenty of time. He knew the high salary offered for this position would bring in the right person. In the meantime, Alisa would be the baby's caretaker. To begin his search, he found a reputable 'head hunting' agency specializing in what he needed and hired them. He solicited all his friends and acquaintances throughout the country that he knew, who were nutritionists, chiropractors, sports medicine doctors, or the like, for possible candidate referrals.

Boy, did they respond! Some of his friends, jokingly, asked if they could apply. So the process of finding prospects didn't take long at all. It was going to be the interviews that would be the time factor. This would be one of the most important parts of the plan. *She had to be perfect!*

The third part of the plan was to create the physical facilities to make this plan happen. He had his millions already, and he expected millions more to come in from all the legal settlements, which take considerable time. He decided that while his interviewing phase was going on, he would hire an architect referred to him by a friend. He was going to build a huge complex with over forty acres of flat land. The drawings would be complete in a matter of weeks. Eventually, he would live there in an airy, beautiful home with a separate laboratory building for his continuing research, a separate home for his nanny, with rooms enough for a future husband, children, and a second full time nanny assistant. Another separate living quarters building for coaches, employees, and temporary contractors. A full football field with goal posts and a track, a work-out building, swimming pools, jogging trails, basketball courts, a nine-hole golf course, an airfield, and finally, a large beautiful garden area filled with flowers to honor his beloved Jean. A bonus would be given to the contractor building the house if it was completed on time. All of the lands would be put to use for his plan.

The tutor candidates applying for the position coming through the agency had already been thoroughly interviewed. The other candidates were instructed to send their resumes directly to Jason's e-mail. There were many more candidates than expected. Jason set his first parameters in his first pass and narrowed it down to fifty. The next set of parameters got the number down to his goal of ten candidates. Now the personal interviews would begin; meetings face to face.

Along with all the physical attributes and educational background he wanted to feel their temperament, their point of view, the hard or softness in their voice. How they viewed the world, their beliefs about religion, politics, and anything else not normally asked at an interview, that could tell him more about the person's inside, their feelings and opinions, anything he and the candidate would have in common to casually talk about. He did this to find the warmth, trust, and love needed for this position. And most of all, he had to *like* her. All ten were attractive, some beautiful, and two striking. He was, after all, a man, but he was smart enough to know that he couldn't let those male feelings get in the way of his plan.

Remember, the focus must stay on the child. He would remind himself whenever his ego-mind would produce thoughts in the *other* direction. Jason's personal life would have to wait.

It took four previous interviews, and on the fifth, he hired her. Her name was Rachael Maccabee. She was one of the striking beauties. She was born an Israeli, an offspring of an Israeli diplomat. She was now an American citizen in her mid to late-twenties, with impeccable credentials, had won a silver medal in Olympic swimming and served in the Israeli Army. She earned a master's degree in nutrition, minored in languages as an undergraduate, graduating with the high honors, could speak fluent English, Spanish, Hebrew, Arabic, learned French and German while living in Paris with her parents. She was currently taking Russian language classes, and had all the physical attributes Jason was looking for. She had a clear, soothing, soft-spoken voice that could be listened to forever. She had previously worked in the United States as a nutritionist and personal trainer (Jason had contacted some of her patients/clients) for a company specializing in weight loss. She had a boyfriend, and their relationship was beginning, so marriage was a long way off. She loved children and wanted to have her own someday.

At their last interview, before he offered the position to her, he had thoroughly described her position and duties. She would move into her private residence as soon as the house was ready. As soon as she was settled in the living quarters, she would hire an assistant from the remaining interviewed candidates, who would also live in a separate part of the house with its own private entrance, kitchen, etc. He made it clear that Rachael would be responsible for hiring, supervising, training, maintaining high standards, and accounting for the finances and record keeping of the assistant. If the person Rachael wanted to hire had already been in Jason's top ten, it would not be necessary for him to re-interview the candidate. He knew that when he hired Rachael Maccabee, she would find the right person to be her assistant on her own. The play was written, the stage was set, the beginning actors were in place, and the Created Plan would begin!

Part Four: The Early Years

Chapter XV

It took a few years to settle all the lawsuits, but finally, with the previous millions he had already acquired through his successful investments, Jason was now a multi-millionaire. When he contracted with his architect to design his 40-acre complex, it was based on a $40 million budget limit, a million an acre, when privately, he estimated a $45. He knew there would be changes and mistakes that no one could predict. In that sense, he was smart. In the builder's contract, there was a clause allowing the contractor to earn bonuses for meeting or beating certain conditions that were advantageous to both parties. It all went fairly well. It took many, many subcontractors to complete it, but nine months after the first shovel went into the ground, Jason, his Grandson, and two female employees moved into their new homes. Later, more service employees would be hired to manage the huge complex. The estate was far from any big city and the entrance was gated with a notable amount of security cameras. Rachael was beaming because the swimming pools were completed, while some of the fields for the sports complex had not yet been started. Some were still in the construction phase, but there was no urgency to have these immediately, as there was plenty of time for little baby Stephen to grow up before he would use any of them. And he did grow!

After his first two years on earth, Stephen had learned to speak a few words in different languages and was walking and consuming low doses of the formula, which was Jason's secret from anyone else. In one of their usual early morning briefings, Rachael and Jason discussed Stephen's isolation from the outside world as he had never played with other children his age. Agreeing that it would be very healthy for him to spend time with other tots, Rachael did research to find a high quality preschool nearby, made her recommendation to Jason, and was given the approval to enroll his grandson. The preschool's administrators understood that because of Stephen's strict diet and use of different languages, Rachael or her assistant Suzanne would be allowed to stay at the school to assist him. Instructions had been given that they were the only ones to feed Stephen's daily portions of formulated vittles, and that was never to be violated. Those instructions were written in both Rachael and Suzanne's contracts. The tutors believed that the formula was a special formulation of vitamins, minerals, vegetables, fruits, and proteins (and it was.) and had no reason to believe otherwise. Jason had thought out everything possible to execute his plan with as much privacy and precision. He had to be a perfectionist to make it all work.

At three years old, Stephen was given his first football. Grandpa would start explaining what it was and how to kick, throw and catch it. Now at five years old, having had his grandson watch many college and professional football games on TV and feeding him his 'Hercules Formula,' Jason knew how strong Stephen H had become and how football was beginning to become his grandson's favorite game. After attending preschool up to five, his private tutored formal education would begin with Rachael. He would be too strong to go to any school and play with other children his age because of the possibility of injuring someone. In addition, Stephen needed to keep speaking the languages Rachael had already taught him.

Along with his diet, strict regimentation for his education and physical activities would now be implemented. Jason would start employing retired professional football and baseball players and coaches to teach Stephen everything they knew. At five years of age, he looked ten and could speak three languages fluently. Being home in the middle of nowhere wouldn't draw any attention. In addition, all of Jason's hired guns would have to sign a contract of strict confidentiality, gagging them and legally preventing them from saying anything about their contract, work performed, etc.

Rachael and Suzanne's day began at 5:00 AM, first waking their student while delivering a glass of water with lemon. He had already learned the importance of personal hygiene at five years old. When it came to brushing his teeth, he was taught to use just a small amount of toothpaste, just enough to do the job to keep his teeth clean and healthy, explaining that using any more was considered wasteful. He would then dress, as Alisa had already laid out his exercise clothes the night before, and he already knew how to tie his shoe laces. At 6:00 AM, Rachael would attend her daily morning meeting at Jason's office while Suzanne took Stephen for his daily calisthenics and jog. The exercises were designed to be short and fast with lots of variety so that her young charge wouldn't get bored. The initial jogs also were very short, then to the playground for swinging, monkey bars, tumbling, sliding, and a morning visit with his friend chimpanzee, Hercules. Rachael ensured that each day, she was speaking a different language to her student. Next, Rachael would take the child to the swimming pool for a swim lesson, off to the shower, and then breakfast, where there was always an opportunity of teaching another word or two; education, education, education.

Each day Jason would devote time to Stephen, whether it was a morning jog, in the classroom with Rachael, physical activity with a coach, or breakfast or lunch, Jason was there encouraging his grandson. And after Jason had the dream with visions of the Statue of Liberty, the American flag, and a portrait of George Washington, he decided to read more about the man from Virginia and read he did. He found a new respect for the man who delivered this country's freedom. And to ensure Stephen was fully knowledgeable about the father of our country, after each dinner meal, Grandpa would always hold up his three middle fingers of his right hand, making a W and mention a related historical fact about the First President, instilling George Washington's ideals into his grandson!

Jason knew the dinner table was where the real deeper learning happens. The unconscious ingestion of information into the subconscious, especially at the dinner table, is where future unrecognized 'ISMS' lives either in love or fear. This is why Jason, Stephen, Rachael, and Suzanne would spend every evening together discussing the day's events and the next day's programs of education and physical activities. This is where table manners, good listening habits, and courtesy were learned. It was a great conversation where everyone could speak openly, be heard and understood, and ask questions about the current topic. A daily structured environment of healthy eating and hygiene, devotion to exercise, good learning techniques and communication, and respect and love for himself and others had been repetitiously fed into Stephen's subconscious and muscle memory in his very early years. As Stephen grew older, all those positive feelings of support and encouragement by his tutors and coaches led him to a point where positive thoughts and love would always present themselves automatically, feeling natural, even joyful. He began to believe that he was being brought up differently from other kids and that there was a purpose for it, which he suspected but didn't know. He knew other kids went to schools with lots of other students and that he appeared physically larger than his age. He also knew he lost his mother, father, and grandmother to a car accident, but there were no details, that, would come later. His grandpa, Alisa, Rachael, and Suzanne were his only family. Jason ensured that Stephen knew what needed to be known at each stage of his grandson's life. Timing is everything, and it made no sense to divulge things that Stephen wouldn't understand prematurely. It was how his grandson would learn the game of football, slow, unnoticed, undetected growth, one position at a time. That's how Hercules grew, one minutia amount of formula every day, undetectable!

A little over three years after being hired by Jason, Rachael was ready to marry her boyfriend, a Navy pilot, Rob Lehman, who ultimately would be assigned to aircraft carriers. Knowing they would not be spending a lot of time together, they got married anyway, took a short honeymoon, and then moved into their new house on the complex. He was gone in no time. She would get used to it and was alright with it. On his last leave, Rachael got pregnant, and when Stephen was nearly four years old, a baby girl, Jessica, was born to the couple. When Rachael took time off for the baby and vacation times, Suzanne, who was already teaching

Stephen some math, reading, and computer classes, would take over full responsibility for Rachael's duties, including the morning meetings with Jason. This was all anticipated, coordinated, and well-executed. Jason knew planning was everything. That's what successful people and organizations do and accomplish goals over a long time. Jason had pledged to himself five years ago when Jean had passed on, and he began his plan that it would take a long time to bring the world someone on the side of 'good', someone who would stand up and fight evil, mad religious fanatics, government corruption, and the likes.

This pause for Rachael's baby was good for Stephen. Suzanne emphasized other languages she knew and did things slightly differently but maintained the daily schedule and structure. Stephen learned that there were differences between the two and many similarities. He was shown that there is more than one way to get to the same end. Ever since Stephen was three weeks old, his grandfather had guided him through the early stages of life where all children learn patterns of love and fear. Jason had chosen well when he hired Rachael, who hired Suzanne Parks. They were great role models, full of love, laughter, and positive attitudes. Without having a mother or father, Stephen was taken care of by the best. Jason didn't have to concern himself about taking care of Stephen; at least one of them was always with his grandson every day. What a huge load off his mind! Alisa was always at his house all day, Monday through Friday, for their laundry, housekeeping, and meal needs and always left something for the weekends. Now that Stephen was a young boy, Saturdays were used to concentrate on football.

In the early morning, it would be exercise and a jog with Grandpa, then a light breakfast and a walk to the football field where they would play catch until the coach arrived. This was the first coach ever to work with Stephen. The first time the coach arrived, he couldn't believe the setup of the complex, especially the indoor pool and gym and the size of the football field, with a track and all the equipment.

After meeting with Jason, the coach said, "Jason, you take football seriously!" Jason smiled widely and replied, "Coach, I love the game and want to teach my grandson everything about it. I brought you here because you were highly recommended by the head coach of my Alma Mater. You will notice that Stephen is young but large for his age and maybe even stronger than some of the older boys you coach. When you determine that he can play with the older boys, I'd like to bring him to your Pop Warner team's practices. I won't be sending him to school for a few years, and I'd like him to play football with older boys. That way, you can practice and teach at the same time, and then when he becomes eligible, I'd like my grandson to play in those junior leagues. He needs proper tackling, catching, blocking, and running techniques to learn to play safely. I think we can easily come to a compensation agreement for your services. Can you do it coach?"

"It looks interesting, Jason. I think I'm going to enjoy it, thanks. When do we start?"

Chapter XVI

It began with Stephen's football learning and training experiences. At a very young age of five, he would begin to develop the game's knowledge and disciplines he would hold for the rest of his life. Stephen's first coach, George Brown, was a quarterback coach in college and professional leagues. He retired with a pension and decided to offer his coaching experiences to kids in the junior divisions. The coach knew all about football, but specializing in coaching quarterbacks was most challenging. But now, so early in this boy's journey, he could teach good techniques and habits without undoing any old bad habits. This sense of being aware of a clean newness for a teacher gives rise to hope and optimism, which gives rise to energy, enthusiasm, and urgency. Coach Brown would be an excellent start. When completed, the coach presented his plan to Jason. The two men met in Jason's office. They spent hours going over the plan, which included time scheduling for individual training sessions, team practices, reviewing videos of televised games, and critiques of videos of Stephen's performances.

First, the game had to be learned, teaching objectives and goals to score touchdowns. There were many understandings and agreements discussed between the two men, one of which was, in so many words, that Stephen was and had been on a very strict diet of formulated nutritious foods all his life with no fast foods, white flour, or processed sugars and therefore would be slightly larger and stronger than his average player, and that safety, for both Stephen and especially the other players, was a priority, and therefore it was agreed that decisions concerning safety would always be on the side of caution. Jason wanted Stephen to play football with other kids so that Stephen could learn about his own feelings and emotions, as well as those of the other players experiencing interaction with other kids, which would lead to the development of new friendships. Also another agreement between the two was that while playing with other kids, there was to be no favoritism one way or the other. Stephen was to be treated the same as all the other boys. Private training on the complex, however, was obviously the opposite.

As time passed, instruction and critiquing of football went on throughout the year, but when baseball and tennis seasons arrived, Stephen's time would be split among the sports. Again he would have private coaches for those sports. The coaches were previous professionals, now teaching their skills to other students, highly recommended to Jason from reliable sources. All teachers would supply plans just as the football coach had, and all training plans were always thoroughly discussed between the coaches and Jason. Communication, agreements, and follow-up were innate awareness within Jason. Every detail needed to be discussed and nailed down so there was a clear path to run on. Everything had to go seamlessly if this plan was going to work. Unforeseen obstacles would inevitably appear, sometimes with unintended consequences, but they could usually overcome with understanding, that is, proper communication. That's why all of Jason's documents and contracts were in writing without legal language and with a clause above the signature line that informs the signer not to sign the document if there is anything that is not thoroughly understood. In that way, if it became necessary in the future to review something, there it was in writing!

Stephen was a fast learner, and he absorbed everything. Beginning at six years old, after Coach Brown had started teaching quarterback training to Stephen, the Coach started teaching him the other twenty-one positions of the game. They would spend months developing each one until the student fully understood how to play it and the importance of successfully executing the mission of the position. Jason and the coach knew that when Stephen learned what each player spot was about and how it was tied into the quarterback's actions, the Grandson would know his opposing team's actions and reactions and thus allow him to make better decisions and adjustments while playing quarterback.

Knowledge is power!

The more you know about something, the more confidence, and power you gain. The coach and Jason were both strong advocates of muscle memory training, visualization, drilled automatic reactions, and of course, practice, practice, and more. All the coaches were amazed at Stephen's strength, speed, and endurance at such a young age. They were all pleased with their results, for the young boy was progressing much better than expected. Stephen would also be able to learn to use either hand to throw a football or swing a tennis racket as well as a bat from either side of the plate. At one point, they talked among themselves about the boy's unusual strength and the special diet. They knew that Jason was an accomplished, celebrated nutritionist, but they could only surmise the possibilities. When they discovered that they all had confidentiality clauses in their contracts prohibiting them from discussing their contractual work at the complex, they thought it best to stop the speculations and discussions. They were all responsible thinking coaches who valued trustworthiness. "Stephen's diet was Jason's business, not theirs," they all agreed, and that subject would never be brought up again.

Five years before, when Jason decided to create his plan, he made an unconscious decision that would change his attitude, his so-called method of operation. His father taught him to *beware of big government, its secrets, lies, and corruption.* He grew to learn that the government inevitably had to lie. In cases that might cause a national panic, government officials were instructed to make statements that could be true or not to keep the public calm. Statistics that favored the government's position could be manipulated and published without mentioning any unfavorable results. Studies that the government would initiate and conduct unfavorable to the political party in power could go unpublished or appear in some newspaper or government document, buried deep inside the publication so as not to be found or appear important. A big controversial bill passed by Congress would be touted as a success, but to get it passed, there are usually many so-called minor trade-offs attached to the bill which people never know about because it might have killed the bill. These additional legislative proposals usually have nothing to do with the bill's main purpose and are kept quiet so that Congress could sneak them through without notice. The average person would say that withholding information is as unethical as lying. And as we have seen in Vietnam and Iraq, where certain incidences may or may not have occurred, the government put America to war. These practices are not at all uncommon in all governments. However, to make a positive change to fight these corruptible practices is a case of either fighting city hall from the outside, without using political influence, money, or favors, or the opposite; using the same tactics the government uses, that is, 'fight fire with fire'. Jason may have been unaware that he was using government tactics, such as asking Zack Blankhardt for a favor obtaining the research equipment from the government for his own benefit, which could appear to be using political influence. Also, without ever removing one page of research from the laboratory, Jason memorized all the research details and documented it on his personal home computer. Many see this as dishonest, untrustworthy, or unethical, even though the doctor's intentions were founded upon the idea of not trusting the government to use the formula for misguided or devious intentions. And last, a big one, the decision to use the formula on his grandchild without it ever having been previously used on a human. Though the intentions were to create something good in the future, it most certainly could be interpreted as immoral, to say the least! However, Jason's idealist intention that his formula is used only for good purposes appeared to him to be a courageous act, which leaves the question of ethics and morality in one's actions to accomplish one's goals.

My, my, how we are all created perfectly imperfect!

Chapter XVII

Jason's life was mostly filled with his grandson's life. His love life was suspended for many years. Continuing to communicate with Jean at nighttime about their grandson while falling asleep kept him emotionally attached to her. This kept his thoughts away from courting or having any romance in his life. He devoted every moment to execute the plan he felt was ordained. "After all," he thought, "wasn't it exceptional circumstances from the time I was introduced to nutrition in high school until the loss of my beautiful Jean that my whole life was being prepared for this challenge? What could be more important?" These first years he worked longer hours than he ever had before. He was always at the construction site while his homes and other enormous facilities were being built. His laboratory was an important building adjacent to which he had to build a secure outdoor living area for his chimpanzees with plenty of space to roam. When he wasn't with Stephen, Rachael, or Suzanne, he always had things to catch up on, attending to finances and investments, his lab work, biotech technical journals, and seeking coaches and employees for his complex, maintenance, etc., just to mention a few. It was really mundane stuff, but overall exciting for Jason to see the steps of progress made from a dream to make it a reality. Once he had made his decision, there was no wavering from it, no complaining when things were not delivered on time or receiving the wrong item, or dealing with subcontractors' mistakes or slowness. Jason had no outbursts when things went wrong, and he vowed to keep his cool by saying to himself: "It's expected. Fix it and move on." Anyone who didn't know him before would soon learn how meticulous he was, and eventually, everyone learned that if he didn't like the results of your work, it would be re-done at your expense, but he was always fair. He would have the main contractor and another subcontractor look at another sub's work and see if it was acceptable to them before deciding to accept it or have it re-done. Common sense would always rule. He learned or rather was gifted common sense from his father. When he was a young boy, he always believed that everyone had common sense, as if it came from the Creator's body and soul. Boy, did he learn the truth! He also learned that to even start on an adventure or take the first step in the dark, creating something no one else had ever done, took confidence. He really believed that all his previous laboratory experience in his previous project with the government would allow him to reach his goals. Even though he could not do so for the project, he truly believed in his dreams with Jean and his abilities to complete what he started. His day-to-day actions showed confidence and mental strength. He believed that a baby was an empty computer, and the infant's brain would act the same as a computer; *Goodness in, goodness out*, or the opposite, *garbage in, garbage out*. Positive supporting actions and responses by the parent or teacher go a long way in creating self-esteem, a positive attitude, and respect for human life. Always saying 'I love you' to a child at any age produces loving responses and, as mentioned previously, becomes ingrained within memory by repetition and eventually becomes automatic and self-believing; thus, as a child grows to an adult, their first immediate response to questions or situations will come from 'love' instead of 'fear'. Teaching love produces loving responses, such as seeing the world in light, while fear produces negative reactions and words that paint the world as dark. Plain and simple, by teaching love, fear is blocked out, as both cannot coexist at the same time. Jason was a strong believer in the psychological benefits of continuous drill and repetition to produce an automatic response. That is precisely what happens to a recruit in military training; drill, drill, drill, so the command is automatically followed without thinking. That is why it was so important to Jason to be constantly aware of what was being said and taught to his grandchild. It had to be unmistakably ***GOODNESS IN!***

Chapter XVIII

Amazingly, with his uncle, retired Senator Richard Blankhardt, as his campaign manager, Zack Blankhardt, now settled down and married with three children serving his second term as a US Senator, was not a corrupt politician as he could have turned out to be. He cared about the country and was a decent man and true representative of his state. Following the series of Jason's tragedies, he had attended all of the funerals and after-funeral invitations to Jason's home. The visits were always short as politicians were busy men, but Jason never forgot those caring words, and their friendship grew over the twenty-two years they had known each other. Jason made a large donation to Zack's campaign, a thank you, a payback if you will, for Zack's past favor and friendship. In one of their breakfast meetings together, Jason learned that all the research documents confiscated by the security company had been summarily destroyed and thought to himself now that Jean was gone, he was the only person in the world who knew of the formula. Because of such frequency of daily use, Jason had already memorized the formula and safely destroyed all the documents. Now there was nothing to show that the formula ever existed!

Over the past five years, Jason and Zack had become good friends. Time was precious between them, for each was always busy with their work. But because Zack knew that Jason was bringing up Stephen in a very sheltered life and environment of tutors and coaches, Zack took a keen interest in Stephen's progress, even though he did not yet know of Jason's plan. However, he did know that Jason still had the chimpanzees, Hercules and Venus, in a huge enclosed area on the complex, the laboratory building, and equipment and that Stephen was eating a healthy, mostly organic, non-processed foods diet, as occasionally Zack and his family would visit Jason and Stephen at the complex on a holiday weekend to catch up on their lives and activities. At her first opportunity to ask Jason about nutrition and diets, especially for her children, Zack's wife, Priscilla, was advised by Jason to remove all the sugared junk food from the entire house to prevent a sugar addiction. During all their socializing, Priscilla would always try to fix up Jason with one of her female friends. After many attempts, Jason decided to accept her offer.

The first time was dinner at a fine restaurant where there would be Jason, his blind date, and the Blankhardts to make it comfortable for all four concerned.

Priscilla's friend, Julia Tressman, was a shapely, beautiful, well-to-do widowed Jewish woman with chestnut-colored hair, a stately demure and extremely well educated and knowledgeable. The evening went very well. Being very nervous initially, Jason allowed Julia to speak openly as he wisely listened. Listening, being more calming than speaking, was his philosophy for reversing his nervousness and allowing him to learn something new, rather than speaking about something he *already knew*! Of course, he had questions to ask and questions to answer, but he was much more interested in learning about her than talking about himself. Zack and Priscilla were wonderful hosts, and the overall experience felt great to Jason, as this was the first time he had spent time with a female companion since Jean had passed. While driving home in Molly, his thoughts were of manly excitement as he recalled his love with his first and only love, the warm physical feeling and peacefulness inside of being alive while sharing life together. His thoughts about the day and his dinner experience would be relived as he closed his eyes to visualize Jean and ask for her approval. The following morning, it was back to business. He wanted time to think about anyone new coming into his life. He knew he had to see her again to explain his circumstances, but he needed time. That day he sent Zack and Priscilla a thank you note along with a note to Ms. Julia Tressman thanking her for a thoroughly enjoyable evening with the hope of seeing her again. In the meantime, Stephen was turning six in a few months and starting a new chapter in his life, already grown from a tot to a boy.

In the first two years after being introduced to football, Stephen wasn't old enough to have any physical contact. It had been mostly watching college and professional sports, football, on TV, and freely kicking, catching, and throwing the football around. The concussion discussions in professional football, as well in colleges, high school, and all other organized football leagues, concerned Jason so deeply that, for the time being, he would allow Stephen, at five years old, to play only flag football (no tackling). He knew it would be a good amount of time before a safer approved helmet could be practical for the average kid to afford because of the amount of testing and more expensive materials to be used, initial startup costs to mass-produce the product, and the amount of *red tape* it would take to acquire official approval. Thus early football was limited mostly to theory and imitating techniques of the best players seen on TV. Even though Jason knew Stephen's added physical attributes could absorb greater impacts than other players, he was also concerned for all other players' safety, especially when the stronger, larger, and tougher Stephen could easily hurt someone else. Throughout those early years, Jason noticed that Stephen never cried or appeared to be in pain, not something that was normal for young boys who played hard and fell down a lot. That left Jason curious about his grandson's pain threshold level!

Part Five: From Boy to Young Man

Chapter XIX

Jason had his work to do, and the months quickly turned into years, and Stephen was becoming a young man before he knew it. Jason had always planned to tell his grandson everything, and now was the time to explain to Stephen about his parents. When Stephen was just starting preschool, he realized he had no mother and father, unlike all the other kids in his class who would be dropped off or picked up at school by a parent. When the question of parents, *why don't I have a mom & dad?* had previously been asked by Stephen when he was three years of age, Rachael responded, "They had an accident, they all died and went to heaven. Your mother was Grandpa's daughter, so you live here in Grandpa's house. Someday when you get older, your grandpa will tell you all about your mother, father, and grandmother." Alisa, Rachael, Suzanne, and his grandpa were the only ones he knew as his family, but now Stephen had the knowledge that someday he would find out about his birth parents. Jason didn't really know scientifically when it was the right time to discuss important matters with a child. He would confer with his team, use common sense, and carefully review the words he would use to convey his stories. So it was one evening at the age of eight, Stephen sat quietly on the couch in the sunroom holding a football, surrounded by his adopted family. Then Jason sat down beside him on the couch, put his arm around his grandson, and gave an account of what had happened to Stephen's parents, Susan and Michael Kellogg and grandma Jean, while they looked at precious pictures of their lost loved ones. When it was over and the facts unfolded, there were soft words, sadness, and tears as Stephen discovered why he was so special and different from the other kids in his class. There were lots of hugs and kisses from his family and an assurance that everyone loved him. With tears in his eyes, Stephen went to bed with pictures of his parents, wondering what life would have been like with them had they lived. He cried and finally fell into a deep sleep.

When Stephen had just seen his first Christmas tree at an earlier age, he asked Rachael a question about it. She had responded that it was a time of celebration called Christmas and a story about Santa Claus coming down the chimney in his red suit to deliver gifts to good little boys and girls. At their meeting the following morning, with Rachael and Suzanne sitting in their normal places facing Jason behind his desk, Rachael broached the subject of Stephen's question. There was silence for a few moments before Jason spoke. He began, "This, obviously, is a very difficult subject. We have not, to date, devoted much time to religion, Darwin's theory, The verses of the Tao, or any other related matters. I have purposely waited until it was brought up naturally, as in a child's curiosity of things, and now may be

94

as good a time as any for a discussion of some of those topics. Religion, politics, and personal beliefs are always difficult and have many sides and interpretations. So, after you have listened to what may be called m*y own personal beliefs*, I would like your feedback. If there are any conflicts within your life that would prevent you from teaching Stephen my personal views, you will have an opportunity to discuss your concerns. Shall I move on?" They nodded. "You have probably heard me use the word *Creator*. I mostly use that word instead of God because there are so many ways religions interpret and teach the word 'God'. Yes, I am a scientist, and religion and science have their conflicts, but I believe and have faith in God as the Creator. Faith in a Creator is much different from faith in a religion. That is to say, faith is necessary for religion, but religion is not necessary for faith if that makes any sense. I am not sure how everything exists, nor why. I believe the Creator has created the most magnificent evolution system for the entire universe. Everything is always unseeingly changing. I have read the Tao written long ago by Lao-Tzu and wish to guide Stephen's life in that direction. I would have to go far back in my family tree to explain how my family's religious beliefs have changed over time. So to summarize: some of my previous family trees had been Jewish, and during a dark period of European history, some families, under duress, converted to become Catholic but were not truly faithful.

95

And subsequent generations slowly drifted away from organized religion. By the time I was born, my family believed in God as a higher power within oneself, a belief in God without a religious attachment. Out of that, my father and mother slowly grew spiritual, as did I and later Jean. My spirituality as faith is related to one's soul and the world as universal consciousness. The fact that so many people have perished and will perish in the name of God and religion is a cause of great concern to me. I wish to suggest that my grandson's faith, so to speak, shall be *Goodness, Kindness, and Knowledge,* and that of the Tao. Most important is that we carefully teach him what *Goodness* is and that there is also evil in this world that must be stamped out wherever it exists. Have him learn that the word 'Creator' is also the 'Createe', being everywhere and everything. Teach him to trust nature, and his instincts, respect his miraculously constructed human body as a sacred temple and have tolerance and goodwill toward all other humans. We will be guiding Stephen as he grows to maturity. Everything we teach him will affect his life. He will study religious theology when he can understand it. And after that, he can then make his own decisions about religion. Maintaining a positive attitude, teaching him that nature is goodness all around him, supporting his education and activities, being kind in answering his questions, and being aware that what you do now will greatly affect how he will think and act in the future. If Stephen should ask what religion or faith you are, you may, at your choice, respond to his question. And if he asks further questions about religion or God, you may also respond, as I want him to be aware, not afraid, of any religion or subject. If either of you would like to discuss this matter with me privately, please do not hesitate. My door is always open, as is my mind. As to the theory of evolution," Jason continued, "I believe man has evolved from the sea. We are evolving every day and will continue to evolve. We just can't see it because our lives are insignificant compared to the infinite universe. Hopefully, the world will evolve to become less violent and more forgiving. Nature is a great word, in my opinion. It is the natural order of things. This is a good time for Stephen to see and learn about nature so he can respect its beauty, changes of seasons, and life's evolution of birth and death. Now that everything is on the table, starting tomorrow, let's implement the subject of nature in his studies. Rachael, tomorrow morning when Stephen begins his day, point out the beauty in our surroundings, the sky, trees, etc., so he can begin to become aware of nature, and each day thereafter teach him something new about it. If we can keep Stephen interested and aware, appreciation of nature will follow."

Chapter XX

When Stephen was almost eight years old, Coach Brown and Jason had a meeting to discuss Stephen's introduction to Coach Brown's team, the 10-13 years of age category, and how he would be used in practices and inter-team games for Stephen was too young to play in the junior league teams and too strong and too large for the pee-wee leagues, and this would be the first time Stephen would have physical contact with opposing players in organized football. His formal home-tutored education was certainly up to older boys, except in languages and football strategy, where he excelled, but Jason's grandson didn't know about girls or the local vernacular street talk or places kids go to hangout and many other things that kids don't learn by living in a protected secluded environment, which greatly concerned both Jason and Coach Brown. But, they agreed, after all, aren't those the reasons to have Stephen exposed to organized football and outside relationships?

So when the first day of practice was to begin, Jason knew Stephen would be apprehensive and excited at the same time. New older kids, new coaches, physical contact, it would be all brand new to Stephen. As they were walking toward the football field that day, Jason turned his head toward Stephen and began speaking. "This is a new exciting experience for you. Coach Brown and I want you to know that even though these boys you are about to play with are older than you, with your size and especially your training, you will do just fine. Trust yourself in what you have learned and will be learning, and follow what you have done in your practices. You will probably know more about football than most other boys, but they have already played in other leagues and know one another. It is very important for you to get to know all the other players by being kind and friendly, and *always* extend your hand to another player to help him off the ground, no matter which side he plays for. Stephen, no one knows you yet, so there will be a lot of questions. Answer them to the best of your ability for what you know, and if you don't know the answer to a question, tell them *I don't know*. You have always played football for fun. This is a great opportunity to make new friends and develop new skills, so laugh and enjoy the game." Jason could feel his heart beating as he knew this was the beginning of Stephen's introduction into the 'plan'. Making football friends was a huge part of the overall plan, and no one in the whole world knew it better than Jason.

When they arrived at the field and were greeted by Coach Brown, he introduced some other coaches to Jason and Stephen. After a short discussion, they decided that Stephen would work with some players and coaches to determine his status. While all the coaches were talking, Stephen started walking out on the field, first watching and then joining a group, throwing and catching the football with each other. When Jason finished speaking to the coaches, they all turned toward the field and watched Stephen throw the football. After a few minutes of watching, one of the coaches remarked, "He sure has a strong and accurate arm."

Responding, Coach Brown said, "We're teaching him to throw from both sides, and that will give him additional options." The coaches looked at each other. One of the coaches went to Stephen's group and asked them all to run the length of the football field as fast as they could.

Soon after they all lined up on the goal line, the coach yelled, "Ready? Go," and off they went. Smiling at the finish, ahead of all the other boys, when Stephen turned around to see how far behind they were, he suddenly felt uncomfortable and embarrassed as he looked back at the table of huddled coaches. Before Stephen returned to his grandpa, he waited at the goal line for the other boys to finish and shook each hand as they passed by, saying, "Great run!"

"Yes," thought Jason, "there will be questions, lots of questions!"

When practice was over, everyone was buzzing about Stephen's abilities, which concerned Jason. Stephen, he thought, was not ready to be a standout. Actually, the plan was to stay low-key until it was the right time to do otherwise. Immediately, Jason turned to Coach Brown and whispered, "We need to talk." They walked over to the player's bench and sat down as the rest of the crowd was beginning to gather their gear and head out. Jason paused in thought before he spoke. "Here is what I suggest. I have an idea that Stephen can be a 'practice quarterback' when the team practices on your field. Then for the physical contact part, he can learn to play all the other positions. You know, Coach, I am a nutritionist and have fed him a special, practically sugarless diet all of Stephen's life. Compared to the other boys who are even older, I don't think he even knows how strong he really is. You know how hard he practices, works out with weights and runs. It's our job to introduce the violent part of football very slowly and carefully. Proper blocking and tackling techniques need to be reinforced when they go astray. If we can get your team's coaches to use my field for game practices, we can help Stephen begin to learn what football 'feels' like without kicking up too much dust, so to speak. What I mean is, at this time, we need to bring Stephen in softly and quietly into the football world and treat him just the same as the other players. What do you think, Coach?" Coach Brown agreed to the idea of teaching Stephen the physical part of football. He could now teach his gifted student all the other football positions and, over time, finally get to coach what he liked the most: quarterbacking.

Chapter XXI

When Stephen was very young, he visited Hercules every day. They quickly became friends, and when Rachael felt it was the right time, he was allowed to go inside Hercules fenced-in area with the groundskeeper to see how Hercules would react to Stephen. They discovered an amazing gentle attachment. Soon after, little Stephen learned to jump and swing with Hercules like a 'Boy Tarzan'. By ten years old, Stephen could jump, swing, and move so fast that he could almost keep up with the chimpanzee. Over the next four years, Stephen did not play league games against opposing teams because of his age restriction. But when he played at *his* field, his usual position was a quarterback. On his field, now with amazing skills, he learned about football's physical tactics, and did he ever love it! He would often fill in at other positions so a line coach could pull out a player to watch from the sideline, and then the coach would say: "On the next play, watch what Stephen does." Stephen, who was so strong, talented, and knowledgeable about football, soon became known to his teammates as the coach's coach. Since he didn't play against other teams, his phenomenal abilities were only known to the team's players and coaches. A short time after joining the team, being the toughest, smartest, and fastest player, he soon displayed skills on the field that no one had seen before, such as

102

catching the ball up in the air with one hand, hurtling players that would go low when he carried the ball and throwing the football equally efficient from either side of the field using either hand. When his teammates would look stunned at his abilities and then compliment him, he would very humbly say 'thanks' and give them a *high five* to be just another player on the team. He soon blended into the team and was treated almost like the team's mascot and coach's assistant on league game days, just another regular guy at a football game. Wisely, Jason liked it that way. The timing was everything; show your hand too early or too late, and you have lost the right moment!

As time passed and Stephen ended his twelfth year of life, he was still in the junior league but now in its highest division. Jason now planned on Stephen going to a special private prep school for training football students 15-17 years of age for college. The first thing Jason did was to have Coach Brown go to the schools and meet all the coaches, scout their various football programs and report back. He did. Brown liked the coaching staff and their teaching techniques at a campus called Russell Prep School. An institution specifically designed for athletic students looking for an elite education and is known for its football greats who graduated from there. Most of their previous graduating players received scholarships to big universities or Ivy League colleges. Right after Jason had made his decision to choose Russell Prep, he immediately met with Rachael. At that meeting, Jason exposed some very confidential information about Stephen's future plans; playing professional football.

Jason needed to inform Rachael of that fact so she could understand why Stephen would be attending this particular prep school and explain how important this change would affect everyone because the school was located in New England, far away from the complex. They discussed that even though Stephen was now enormous for his age and far beyond his years in education and football, he was still only thirteen and that Stephen needed to live off-campus with Rachael as guardian, continuing to be his tutor and surrogate mother. They decided that they would speak to the head of the prep school and see if all parties could be accommodated. They did. After that meeting, it was agreed that Stephen, being younger, would be allowed to reside off-campus with Rachael. The next step would be to find an apartment near campus and get them all ready for the new school year, including Rachael's daughter Jessica, who, now at the age of nine, would continue to be home-schooled by her mother. Jason would remain home at the complex, attend the school's football games and visit as much as possible. Coach Brown would visit practices weekly and attend all their scheduled games. Jason told Coach Brown that it was too soon to expose Stephen's abilities at this young age, so before a final decision was made, Coach Brown was again sent to the school to discuss Stephen's current and future roles as a player. Following Jason's directions, Brown convinced the head coach and coaching staff to use Stephen only as a *backup* quarterback (they would later find out how unbelievably good he really was) and use him in other positions during games. The exception would be that he could be used as quarterback near the end of a game if they were behind or tied and he was needed to win the game. At his young age, looking like a big 16-17-year-old football player, Stephen would begin his quest to play in the Professional Football League.

While Stephen was going through his boyhood years developing into a young man, Jason's life was also full. He continued to vigorously monitor his chimpanzee, Hercules. Every test would become more important than the previous test because of time. Hercules was on the special formula until he reached the age of seventeen. Over those seventeen years, the amount of formula was ever so slightly increased until a peak dosage was reached at age sixteen. That was when the amount of formula was stabilized to the same daily dosage for one year. So before Stephen first started playing football in the junior league, Hercules had been on the formula for seventeen years when Jason stopped it. With no further dosage, there would be less worry about an overdose that killed other test animals. He looked very carefully for any changes in the cells, blood, or visible side effects. It was important now to determine if strength and growth would be maintained or start to drop off. Jason didn't really want an obviously noticeable giant. He wanted Stephen to have a large muscled torso, weighing about 240-250 pounds, standing at about 6'4, and possessing outstanding speed, agility, and power that would take multiple opposing players to bring him down. He believed that looking too huge or appearing to have some kind of superpower would be very freaky or suspicious, something Jason absolutely did not want! But he knew he could not control everything. He continued taking and evaluating the periodic test of Stephen and Hercules and systematically monitored their strength, height, and weight. But one of the things Jason couldn't measure or predict was Stephen's human emotions. How can feelings be measured in a human? Therefore, Jason had to watch for any change in temperament or actions that did not appear natural or normal. Up to this point in time, because of the formula, Stephen was never physically injured. If he got hit, he didn't feel much pain either. However, he hadn't played in many games in his early years and really was never truly tested, especially blocking or tackling opponents. Now playing with the older, larger boys, things could be different.

Another unusual thing was that Stephen noticed he never got sick as other kids did, and Grandpa would always say, "Because you don't eat processed sugar. The more unnatural sugar you eat, the sicker your body becomes. If your system has too much sugar that goes unused, it stores it as fat, changing your metabolism, making the rest of your body work harder with more unnecessary weight that reduces the efficiency of your body functions." Stephen listened intently to his grandfather's repetitive words, more convinced than ever that healthy habits lead to a stronger, happier life.

Stephen's grandfather had first amassed a small fortune by using the funds received from life insurance policies and corporate legal payouts received from his litigation settlements. He invested those funds in startup biotech companies of friends and referrals he knew who were excellent research doctors that had created great businesses. He did a lot of research on the companies on his own and invested as an insider before they went public or got bought out by a bigger company. When he could cash out from a company, he would then look for another company or two to re-invest. That way, he was always ahead of the curve by owning companies doing nuanced research. After many years of investing, Jason became a multi-millionaire, investing in stocks of large dividend-paying corporations, tax-exempt bonds, and treasuries. This was to maintain a steady cash flow to fund all his operations at his complex. It took a lot of money and time to keep his plan viable, and it was no easy task. If he hadn't devoted the time to it, he certainly would not have been as wealthy as he was. He still left little time for himself. He continued to see Julia Tressman whenever he could. She took a great interest in Stephen, and Jason felt very comfortable around her, with conversation coming easy between the two. He was not yet ready to propose to her because he was still heavily involved with the everyday workings of his plan. Now one of the biggest concerns for Jason at this stage in the plan was keeping a lid on Stephen's abilities to avoid attracting any attention. Everyone in Stephen's 'immediate family' knew he was consuming a nutritional formula and other healthy eating habits. But Jason didn't want to offer any information to any future journalistic 'snoopers' who might investigate Stephen's special diet. Jason knew that the subject of nutrition would inevitably be brought up. From the beginning, he knew that ordering and receiving items used in the formula must leave no trail, especially the particular names and amounts of vitamins and minerals, catalysts, and of course, a secret pulverized powder that had to be delivered to an untraceable private PO Box number, under an unconnected business name and picked up by the complex manager in brown paper packaging.

Part Six: Stephen's Teenage Years

Chapter XXII

Now that Stephen and Rachael were away at school, Jason felt alone. Yes, he still had Alisa, his housekeeper, and Suzanne, who now would be assisting him in running his complex and his finances, but it wasn't the same as it was with the whole family together. Even Coach Brown wouldn't be around much now that he was spending time at the prep school in New England, so it was very quiet at the complex. It gave Jason time to think of what had been accomplished and what had yet to be done to reach his goals. One day he thought how unlucky he had been losing almost all of his family, but at the same time, how lucky he had been in having Stephen as a grandson and, to date, having no major setbacks to his plan. "How ironic," he thought, "isn't that always the way? The universe always seeks balance. For every loss, there is a gain. For every *yes,* there is a *no*. For every action, there is a reaction. And for every reaction that doesn't result in a positive response, could there have been a pro-action that could have prevented the reaction? What pro-actions do I need to think about that will prevent an action or reaction from having no unintentional consequences," he thought to himself. "I must always think far ahead. There will be unstoppable journalists chasing Stephen when he begins his football career. I must plan out the right course," as his mind drifted to a new subject, Stephen's military service to his country.

Part of the overall plan was to have Stephen serve in the US military. Not just as a staff or support officer but as a member of an elite combat unit. Even though never being tested, Jason believed that Stephen's body was not 'bulletproof' but much stronger than an average human being, increasing the odds of coming home safely. He actually wanted Stephen to be in an active unit in America's foreign war zones to experience combat in special operations. He wanted Stephen to train with the best, giving Stephen a better chance of surviving and for Stephen to see for himself what war and fighting terrorism really was, the suffering and destruction, how other people in the world live, and how they cope with their misfortune. Jason knew you couldn't read about those terrible atrocities and *feel* the pain without being there to experience it, live it, first hand! He knew he was gambling with his grandson's life. However, he trusted himself. He believed in what he had learned through many years of research and experimentation. He had devoted his entire life to it. And even though he wasn't absolutely *sure*, he still felt it was necessary for Stephen's career and for the plan to succeed. He knew there would be lots of questions from his staff that needed to be answered. He had his own questions! The first question was: how would Stephen react to the suggestion of postponing his football and college career to serve his country? When, and at what age? What about the interruption of Stephen's football career at this early age? Could he be as good after his service? Jason had to search his soul on the subject. "Way ahead," Jason thought, "I have to plan every move way ahead of time, and I must remain positive all the time." He knew, once again, that all obstacles had to be overcome to accomplish his ultimate goal!

It was tough at the beginning for Stephen. He had not attended school since preschool. It was a big change in his life, and he would have to adapt. He would be exposed to social drinking and eating, and girls! He would now be evaluated with tests and grades. He was first noticed for his boyish looks, but soon that was overlooked because of his football skills and prowess. As always, his first task was making friends with his teammates and coaches. That was easy; he had already had a lot of previous experience in the youth leagues. At school practices, he would always notice when Coach Brown showed up at the field and knew that after practice, Brown would critique his performance and consult with the coaching staff on a cordial, friendly basis, allowing the coaches to believe that he was just an interested spectator of the team. He would never question their decisions or authority. Coach Brown was quite good at what he did, never making a big deal about anything; keeping everything *low-key*. That's why he and Jason got along so very, very well.

The teenage years are so important to a young male teen. It's when they see flaws in their family they want to get away from, the beginning of thinking of being free and independent, thus rebelling and acquiring new friends and ideas, some good and others not so good. Now, the professors would be putting out information to the young minds. In this progressive prep school, students were encouraged to think a lot more on their own and, in turn, produce many more questions for them to ponder further. Jason believed that any kid with proper guidance, support, and encouragement could be taught to utilize rebellious energy positively, with the appearance that the child chose on their own. Jason's tutor and counselor, Rachael, an impeccable surrogate mother, and teacher, was now the most important person in Stephen's life. Stephen acquired a superior education planned and administered by Rachael. He was far, far ahead of his class. Together, Rachael and Stephen selected the classes and drew up the weekly schedules as Rachael did not want to dictate rules and laws to Stephen. She worked with him to explain options, both intellectual and from the heart. She was kind and reassuring in Stephen's decisions and watched his body language and energy for any change in his attitude, always aware of maintaining a positive frame of mind. Oh yes, in addition, there was this matter of consistently inserting Jason's nutritional mixture into Stephen's meal every day, without fail, until he became seventeen. No one in the world could match Rachael, no one!

Stephen was now in the midst of his teenage years. He was living in the real world for the first time and as a teenager. He never had chores or 'outside' responsibilities except to follow his daily schedules at the complex, which occupied all of his time. His social life was extremely limited, and he had only one true friend he slowly began to confide in, Jessica. He couldn't really talk to someone his age about his lifestyle or his thoughts because he had no equals. His closest friend had become Jessica, and since she was three years younger and the daughter of his tutor, having her as a confidant would begin only now, slowly, as they left the complex together for Stephen's new prep school.

And as for Jessica, who was now becoming her own person, she would be studying alongside Stephen. In the past, she would watch Stephen from a distance while he was playing football or see him studying in a separate room with her mom. She was like a fixture in the house, keeping quiet and to herself, but she was socially more exposed to other kids than Stephen. Stephen seemed to never have free time as she did. But now, at the ages of fifteen and twelve, living together in the same apartment, Stephen and Jessica were physically closer to each other. And, over the three years of living that way, they began to share their deep inner thoughts with each other. A beginning that would last a lifetime.

Chapter XXIII

Every football player attending the school had someone who whispered in the coach's ear how their kid was great at this or that position, but after a while, coaches didn't hear the words anymore. They would just think, "We'll see." However, what Coach Brown had told the school's coaches about Stephen was quite different. When the first practice was about to begin, Coach Brown instructed Stephen to just slowly and quietly fit into the team, learn the plays and get familiar with the coaches, players, and surroundings.

"Play every position they choose for you just as I have taught it to you. And remember, always make friends without *showing off* your skills," he said to Stephen. "And by the way, while I am on the subject of friends, close friends are those who can always be truthful with each other and without judging each other." Coach Brown was a very close second to Rachael as far as importance in Stephen's life. He would continue to mold Stephen into one of the greatest football players of all time. What Brown knows is that Jason is a well-known and respected nutritionist, an obvious lover of football, a perfectionist, and a man on a mission who has suffered through the loss of his family. The Coach's observation at the complex led him to believe that Stephen is *special*. He is the result of a nutritional genius, a perfectionist who understands the value of eating and exercising properly for maximum efficiency, as witnessed by the results in Stephen's body growth and abilities on the field. He has seen his student grow from a boy to a quality football player for almost ten years now. He knows Stephen like a son. He knows his strength, durability, and speed in addition to football and intellectual knowledge. The Coach was amazed to see his student swing with Hercules with speed and accuracy. He knows Stephen is highly educated and intelligent and has played well at every single position on the field. And Brown knows his goal for Stephen. Over time, all the coaches and players learned how powerful and talented Stephen was. But for now, at Russell Prep, Stephen practiced with the varsity, but because of age limitations, he could only play on the junior varsity with younger players. When he turned sixteen, however, he would be allowed to play on the varsity, playing in every game and position on the field whenever called upon to help win the game, even replacing the quarterback a few times. At sixteen, he did play in every varsity game with his prep school-going undefeated for that year, winning their division in the playoffs, and without drawing much attention to Stephen, except for one person, Mike Glen, a local sportscaster and writer.

On one of Jason's visits to the prep school, a few months after Stephen turned fifteen, Rachael discreetly pulled Jason aside and spoke to him about Stephen's natural attraction and smile to girls as he sees girls with other older football players and experiences his natural feelings for a boy his age. She thought that maybe it was time for Grandpa to talk with his grandson about the birds and the bees. Now that was something Jason didn't have a plan for! He was startled at first. But he knew she was certainly right, and he agreed. Rachael further explained that there is a nearby 'sister' prep school for girls that have chaperoned dances with Stephen's school and that Stephen is allowed to attend. Again, respecting Rachael's good judgment, he agreed. When Jason was ready to sit down privately with Stephen, Jason brought up the subject of girls.

"Is there anything you need or want to know about girls?" There was an uncomfortable moment before Jason continued. "I've noticed that quite a few of your older teammates have girlfriends picking them up at the field after practice?"

"Well, Grandpa," replied Stephen, "I have learned all the technical reproductive biology part from Rachael, but now I am beginning to have some physical *feelings* if you know what I mean."

"I do," answered Jason. "It is normal; it's part of your maturity to becoming a man. It is a very difficult subject to address. May I first suggest that you talk about it in confidence to one or two of your closest male friends and see if they get similar feelings? You can learn a lot from friends who have dated girls. After that conversation, if you still need more answers, come back, and we'll talk again." Stephen understood. He took his grandpa's advice, went to his closest football school friend, an older boy named Aaron Benes, and never had to bring up the subject to Grandpa ever again. Along with newly acquired carnal knowledge, he would learn to dance, go to the co-ed social events, and at sixteen, be allowed to go on chaperon dates with girls from the all-girl 'sister' prep school. Jessica would always quiz Stephen about his dates.

While Stephen was fifteen, playing for the junior varsity and getting prepared to play in the upcoming year, playing with the varsity team would be the only year of true competitive football for Stephen as he would graduate prep school just before the age of seventeen. About the same time as Stephen was starting prep school, there was a local young sportscast announcer named Mike Glen who had covered the prep school team's three previous seasons on a local radio station and got to know all the school's coaches. When the first game of the new season was approaching, the coaching staff became uncontrollably optimistic about the coming season. Mike was the sportscaster for Stephen's first game that day, and when it was over, he understood why the coaches were so optimistic. Not only did Stephen play some quarterbacking, but he also played linebacker, kicked a 60-

yard field goal (a school record), and ran for three touchdowns as a fullback. This was the most exciting football player Mike had ever seen, and he decided right then and there that he would follow Stephen's career! Little did he know that acquiring information about Stephen's past would be so difficult. As the season progressed, the team was unstoppable and won every game on their schedule. After every game, Mike would run out onto the field to interview Stephen but would always be disappointed to find Stephen hustled off the field by a beautiful woman, who could have been his mother, or by an older black man who looked like an old familiar coach. Mike Glen needed to know more about this football player. As far as he knew, the school never had a previous perfect record, and now they were headed to their division finals as favorites.

While kids grow up, notable events in their lives shape their mind and affect their future decisions and actions; some are conscious, and some are learned unconsciously. As mentioned before, what a child feels, hears, and sees at an early age greatly affects their attitude and outlook toward life when they get older. This is because an infant's brain is just starting to gather information, and each time words, phrases, incidents, and the like re-occur or are repeated over and over. The brain learns to recognize a pattern and, over time, begins to react automatically when the pattern is reintroduced to the brain. For example, a daily practice of repeating an instructed order over and over again, such as 'right face', will eventually create an effective automatic immediate response when the soldier turns to the right without thinking about which side of the body is the right side. This 'drilled' learned pattern and automatic reaction is carried into adult life without the person ever realizing why they reacted the way they did. There are so many things we don't know about raising and educating our beautiful children. Children are like empty computers; they become whatever is loaded into their young, innocent brains. Jason's knowledge of *that* fact is the reason Stephen was brought up the way he was! When Stephen was three years old, Jason introduced him to Hercules and Venus. Jason whispered to Stephen, bending low in front of the caged area: "These are Grandpa's friends, and I would like you to become their friend too." At that age, Stephen had so much curiosity it took a very long time for Grandpa to answer all his questions. But that was just fine because, at Stephen's young age, Jason wanted him to learn as much as he could about chimpanzees, feel comfortable with them, and imitate their physical actions to allow Stephen's brain to learn patterns that would produce automatic physical reactions, like a chimpanzee's speed, swiftness, quickness and leaping ability for use on the football field. "If you would like to become their friend, you can visit and greet the chimps right here every day. Use their name and say hello with a big smile, and soon they will get to recognize you and become your friend. Then you will be able to talk to them, and who knows what secrets they can teach you. Watch Hercules jump and move so quickly from tree to tree and see how he looks like he is flying because he is so fast. You will learn just by watching, and someday when you are older, and you can play with Hercules, you will learn the tricks of being fast, spinning in the air, and catching sure-handedly. Would you like that?"

"Yes, Grandpa," Stephen replied excitedly, "new friends." By the time Stephen was five, he was already jumping on a trampoline, spinning in the air, moving like a chimp. Soon Coach Brown would throw footballs to Stephen while he was spinning in the air.

As all lives do, Stephen's life went through *phases*. Through each phase, his routine of exercises, foods that he ate, his classes, free time, etc., would change. Coach Brown researched whatever he didn't know. At each phase of Stephen's life, the Coach had to learn when and what exercises to give Stephen because the Coach wasn't familiar with the torso of a kid as he was with a full-grown 18-year-old college player that he previously had coached, so that he would talk to Jason and Jason's recommended colleagues in the field of health and human growth. He wasn't afraid to discuss his own shortcomings with Jason, a sign of a sure, confident, vulnerable man. In return, he was able to grow his knowledge and be a better coach, and he knew it. To him,

122

Stephen was unusually strong, and he knew when weightlifting began, Stephen would not only learn the regimentation of working out but would be increasing his strength and agility. Brown knew about the chimpanzees that were Jason's pets, and as Stephen grew up to be an incredible football player, making catches that even he, a hall of fame coach, had never seen before, he knew the kid was unique, one of a kind. He often wondered whether Stephen could be part chimpanzee!

No... he thought. *That was impossible!*

Stephen was so occupied in his younger years that he never had to think about anything except what came next on his schedule. He saw his fellow football friends at practices but didn't have the time to get close to any of them until he got to prep school. Entering a prep school for 15-17 year-olds at fourteen was a challenging social issue for Stephen and Rachael. Stephen learned many things but knew nothing about girls, school life, or socializing. He always learned by listening, and this would be no different, except for one thing, he now had a soulmate, Jessica, that he could talk to. How could you know what you don't know? He knew and loved music and music videos because he was exposed to them. Things that he was sheltered from would eventually have to be introduced to him as part of learning, and entering this new school would be the beginning of that learning. And by the time Stephen finished prep school, just before turning seventeen, he had become close friends with a few of his teammates, acquired many other school friends, dated a few girls, and became familiar with his own sexuality by learning from his close male friends who had relationships with girlfriends. He was still innocent but learned an awful lot at prep school besides studies and football! He was falling in love with Jessica.

Rachael was marvelous during those prep school years. Her continuing repeated tenderness, loving care, and rigid schedule went into Stephen's brain to lead him into an adult life of automatic positive responses to the patterns she so consciously created, taught, and imposed. The teacher teaches good habits, and the student learns good habits. Along with becoming disciplined, Stephen would become a learned man of conscience, tolerance, and tenderness, treating all women with respect because of those positive patterns instilled by his grandfather, Rachael, Suzanne, Coach Brown, and even Uncle Zack. But during those tender teenage years, Stephen was learning to become his own man and make his own decisions. While living away from other people and seeing how they go about their daily lives, Stephen began to understand what a secluded and highly controlled life he had led. Soon after he turned sixteen, he got his license and could now drive without having to be chaperoned, giving him new freedom he had never experienced before. He was beginning to taste real life as if he were just another teenager. And that's when Grandpa Jason brought Stephen home to the complex to discuss his future.

Chapter XXIV

Before Stephen got to sending out feelers for colleges he wanted to attend, Jason knew he had to talk with him about suggesting military service after graduating from Russell Prep. It would be a total surprise to Stephen! It would be a difficult conversation because, at the same time Jason wanted him to decide in favor of serving, Jason wanted Stephen to make his own decision, that is, with his guidance. Just after his birthday, they met in Jason's office on his visit home.

"Stephen, tell me everything that's going on in your life. Rachael has informed me that you are now driving and will graduate next spring."

"Well, Grandpa, the team is doing exceptionally well. We're winning more games than ever before, and all the team players are getting noticed by the college scouts. It's going to be fun choosing a school." Stephen replied enthusiastically.

"Turning sixteen is a wonderful time in your life, and I'm glad to hear you're enjoying it. There is, however, a more important birthday at seventeen, and that is what I wanted to discuss with you," said Jason as he continued. "You know I have always encouraged you to play football and eventually play professional football. It has always been a top priority in your life's development. But Stephen, there are other things in life that are more important, and it is best to address them before your new football journey begins."

"I don't understand, Grandpa. I always thought the next step was to go to college and play football. What is more important than that?" questioned Stephen.

Jason looked at Stephen and said, "Service to your country... I am suggesting that you enroll in the military and serve your country, as I believe everyone turning seventeen should serve this country in some capacity."

"Wait a minute, what is this?" Stephen blurted. "I know nothing about the military. I can't believe this. I won't do it!" Stephen protested.

"It's just a suggestion, Stephen. Once you start your college and football career, you may never be able to get to serve your country. You have an obligation to your country, and it's better to get it over with before starting your higher education and career," said Jason.

"What do you mean *I* have an obligation? You never served," argued Stephen.

"I did serve this country," replied Jason.

"Oh, really," said Stephen sarcastically. "You never mentioned it before. Why not?"

"Well, it never came up before, and it was before you were born," replied Jason. "My service to this country wasn't directly in the military. It was a scientific study for the military. I gave fifteen years of my life to this country, and I could never expose my top secret work, and I still cannot..."

Stephen interrupted, "Scientific study? Scientific study? Study of what? Don't tell me Hercules and Venus were involved..."

There was a long pause.

"Oh, no, I'm a freak! I'm a freak, Grandpa, aren't I?" Stephen cried out. "You had me befriend..."

"No, you're not," retorted Jason. "You are not a freak at all! You have grown up with more opportunities than most other kids, but that doesn't make you a freak. There are other kids who are home-schooled, other kids who play football and workout, and others who eat a healthy diet. You do all those things and might be the best at each. And because of that, you are a healthy, intelligent, extremely well-trained, and accomplished football player. You earned it! Yes, I started your life with nutritious food without additives and sugar, and you grew big and strong. I knew your social life and other things might suffer. But that sacrifice will pay you back many times," Jason explained.

"What did you give me, Grandpa?" queried Stephen.

"I can never speak of the work I did. It was all destroyed. What I gave you was the result of all that I learned, but only what were all-natural and legal ingredients. No illegal hormones or anything like that. Some were exotic herbs rarely used or newly discovered, but all-natural," replied Jason. "Please do not respond now. You are understandably emotional. Please take time and think it through, and we will talk again."

Stephen got up and started walking to the door when Jason said, "Before you make a decision..." as his grandson turned around to look at him, Jason held up his three middle fingers in the form of a W and continued speaking, "Ask yourself: what would George Washington do?" Stephen raced back to his room, threw himself onto his bed, and silently cried. Never before had he ever questioned his grandfather that way. He couldn't stop his emotions and his negativity. He kept thinking... why? After some time lying on the bed, he thought of calling Jess and asking her to come over so they could be alone to talk.

"I feel like a freak, and I told him that! I cannot believe this!" Stephen said to Jessica after he told her about the conversation with Jason.

"I can't believe it either," said Jessica quietly and continued. "First of all. I see how hard you practice, eat, and study, so Stephen, you are not a freak, and don't ever say it again. But how does he ever expect you to decide on something you know nothing about. Do you?"

"No," he replied. "He expects me to fulfill an obligation to this country and assumes the army will teach me everything I need to know, I guess," Stephen answered. "Hell, Jess, I don't know how I would make it out there on my own, especially without you! I'm really mixed up and scared."

She hugged him and held him, then said softly, "Sometimes we don't know why we do things until after we've done them, and then as we live more of life, we find those answers and understand why those experiences were so valuable."

There was a silence.

"Do you think I should do it, Jess?"

"It's not my decision, Stephen. No matter what you decide though, it will be the right one as far as I am concerned. If you choose to enlist, then when you come back, we can go to college together. That would be fun." She kissed him on the cheek.

Stephen turned to face her and said, "You always make me happy, Jess. How can I go away without you?"

After multiple meetings and questions thinking over Grandpa's proposal of military service, Stephen made his decision. At first, the thought of going off somewhere on his own and doing something he knew nothing about totally scared him. But after deep consideration, Stephen knew that there would be a time when he would have to command his own life and live apart from his family, so he agreed to Jason's request that it was now time to go out on his own to see how the rest of the world lives and serve the country as well. He realized his life would drastically change after graduating from prep school.

Chapter XXV

As a young man at seventeen, Stephen would now serve his country while becoming a 'man'. At a meeting with his intimate family, Jason announced Stephen's four-year commitment to the military: "Two years of active duty training with an elite combat unit, two years of active combat duty, and possibly four years in the reserves. However, the reserves would not interfere with his football career."

The family was shocked at the announcement. Jason knew that the response would be shocking, but he would have to answer their questions: "Why jeopardize Stephen's football career with the possibility of death or getting wounded? And why can't he just serve his time in the regular army, navy or marines, or for that matter, the National Guard?" These questions were not going to be easy to answer just because he knew more about his grandson's capabilities than they knew.

Jason said, "Stephen has proven he is capable of being a leader. Now is his time to learn *how* to become a leader and a man. We will no longer be his guardian or protector. His learning about life won't come from a book or thought but from experiences. He must make his own decisions and become a leader before he goes to college to quarterback a team. He will visit the dark and cruel side to know how fortunate he is to live in this country as a free man.

That is very important because so many of us take freedom for granted instead of earned. Many immigrants who have come to America appreciate freedom more than natural-born citizens because they have lived under fear and tyranny, unlike those citizens who have never served their country. In my opinion and the opinion of many, George Washington, our greatest President, would not have been as great had he not battled for his country's freedom. The tremendous sacrifices that he had endured helped make him 'the father of our country'. He would not have been the man he was if he had not served his country!"

Stephen decided it was time to sit down and talk with his grandfather about the change and new phase of his life. Now at seventeen, he would be alone on his own. What would it be like without his grandpa, Rachael, Suzanne, and Coach Brown? And Jessica? He wanted to feel confident, but he became nervous thinking about going out into the world alone. How would the world treat this inexperienced young teen born with a silver spoon in his mouth, a private tutor, and a personal hall of fame football coach? Could he or anyone know? Was this going to be the way to manhood?

Meanwhile, while all this was happening after prep school for Stephen, Rachael's daughter, Jessica, had turned fourteen years old when Stephen graduated. She also had an elite education as she was also home-schooled by Rachael. Little noticed at this age by anyone except Stephen, she was becoming a beautiful and highly educated woman, just like her mother.

It's not easy getting into the army's Special Forces at seventeen, but it happened for Stephen. Usually, the requirements were three years of prior military service with an outstanding record just to apply, but because of a new program, Stephen and other candidates could go to Special Forces Training School after successfully completing army boot camp first, thus eliminating the three-year wait. Stephen applied and got in on his own abilities without ever knowing anything about weapons, military tactics, or the like. After agreeing to apply to the new army program, Stephen immediately went online to learn all about the rangers and their Special Forces' operations. From that day on, Stephen would follow a strict physical routine to give him confidence when performing all the physical tests. After that, he was on the computer reading about military leaders and their tactics, weapons, and everything else he didn't know. He became more confident about his physical and intellectual requirements but wasn't sure he could ever kill another human being, which gave him some anguish, but that's exactly what he would be trained to do. He never showed it on the outside, but he was scared to death on the inside! He was at the age of rebellion for a normal American boy. He knew nothing about the military. He was brought up to love and live football. He was being privately educated by female tutors. He knew of the military only through reading all about George Washington and the American Revolution, which he knew like the palm of his hand, but this, this would be real life! As time moved on, he would have thoughts about it, and the confidence he had built up in his training and studying began to wane with fear in its place. He would find himself in self-doubt. There's nothing like playing football, a game you have already played, and you know what you are up against. But this was new and unknown, and he surely needed to talk with Uncle Zack.

Part Seven: The Making of a Man

Chapter XXVI

Now just over two years after Ft Bragg, he was peering out from a mountain over an unknown immense valley below him, scouting for the enemy, just a short while after completing his military training and subsequent specialized training in medical emergency treatment (his Special Forces MOS). He was crouched on a mountain ledge with multiple weapons and ammo scattered around him, gathered from his injured Special Ops team, looking through his binoculars for any sign of enemy soldiers and at the same time looking for the rescue chopper to pick up the six-man team whose helicopter had been shot down by an enemy RPG, they never saw coming. The round hit the propeller shaft, and luckily the helicopter didn't catch on fire. It was flying low to avoid radar, making the fall survivable. That was the good part. No fire on board meant that Stephen didn't have to deal with burns, and with no fire blazing, it would be more difficult for the enemy to find them high up on a ridge near the top of the mountain. Stephen was not injured. He had, what appeared to be, some bruises but not severe pain. He attributed it to luck. All the other team members were alive but injured, except the pilot and co-pilot; they had died immediately upon impact as the chopper went down head first, leaving the body and tail of the aircraft pointing up toward the sky like a slanted windmill. This was Stephen's very first live mission, and he never even made it to their objective; not only his first combat mission but also his first encounter with death and human injuries. Because he was well trained, he had acted fast and never had time to think about anything. In his medical training, the dead were always portrayed using dummies; that is how he had to think of the dead men, with no emotion. He was well trained and had to care for his team's safety first. All had broken bones and lacerations, some serious. He first pulled them all out of the chopper, one by one, and then tended to their injuries, resetting and splinting broken bones, bandaging the bleeding lacerations. He found a nearby overhanging ledge with a small cave underneath it, where he relocated all the other five members, carrying each one on his back to the safety of the cave. He then notified his Base Commander of their location coordinates, informing his superior of the incident, approximate location, and the number of dead and injured. His team leader was one of the men who were most injured with multiple fractures, and now Stephen was the only member fit to take charge, so there he was, alone, a greenhorn and now the only one capable of leading the team. "Welcome to war!" he quietly whispered to himself.

He saw no movement anywhere around him. That was a very good sign. "Maybe the RPG came from the other side of the mountain, and the enemy couldn't see or hear the crash," he thought. As he turned and scanned the area, he couldn't help but notice the helicopter sticking out from the mountain. He ran back to the helicopter, quickly searched, and found a camouflage tarp. He made some cuts into the tarp, found some loose brush lying around, twisted it into small bunches, and inserted them into the slits of the tarp he had just cut. Then, climbing up on a boulder adjacent to where the chopper's tail was sticking out, he flung the tarp, covered with brush, over the tail, hoping to give it some camouflage, thinking, "Anything to help to conceal it!" Feeling more confident, he returned to his lookout position and resumed searching for the enemy. He saw nothing. He sat back to rest for a moment and had a strange thought pass through his mind. "How did I survive the crash without a broken bone or laceration," he wondered. That was not the first time he noticed and questioned his physical endurance and resistance to a major injury by impact. He had previously noticed his extraordinary strength and speed playing football, but then he really took notice during basic and advanced training. He was stronger than all the men he trained with. This time, however, he had never been in such a violent crash that hit this hard. This impact could have killed most men, he thought, "But the Rangers are in top shape. That's why they survive! What else could it be that saved me from injury?" he wondered.

Stephen was instantly brought back to the present moment when the team Base Commander's voice sounded in his ear, informing him that the emergency helicopter awaiting just outside the border would pick them up and return to base, the mission being aborted. In the meantime, Stephen spotted some movement in the valley below. Two men in a re-configured pickup truck with a machine gun mounted on it arrived and stepped out with binoculars. Both started scanning the hillsides, probably looking for the downed aircraft. Immediately, he felt his adrenaline rush through his body; his heart began beating fast. He could feel it thumping, and for a few moments, all he could hear or feel was pounding against his chest so hard and loud that he thought his heart would burst out of his chest and disclose his location. But after a short time, feeling like hours to him, he recovered and ensured his binoculars could not be spotted glaring in the sunlight. He waited. The enemy soldiers kept looking. Stephen wondered about the location of the rescue chopper. If it were nearing the crash site, the enemy would surely see or hear it. He contacted the rescue helicopter, quietly whispering into his microphone: "Enemy nearby, stay clear of the mountain until I can determine when you can safely land." He kept his eyes glued on the two soldiers traversing the mountains around him to look for the chopper until finally, they drove away. "Maybe, just maybe, the camouflage worked," he thought. He contacted the rescue helicopter to proceed with the pickup, and soon thereafter, their team and the two dead pilots were aboard. On their way back to the base camp, after he had made his Team as comfortable as possible, receiving gratitude from each man for his actions, he finally sat back, took a deep breath, and thanked his Creator that he was able to do what he did and come out of it alive without a scratch. He mourned the death of the two pilots, wondering how their families would take the dire news. At nineteen years old, this was Stephen's initiation into a live combat experience, including death, even though not one shot had he fired. It will always be remembered; the first time is never forgotten by any soldier who experiences combat!

The night before Stephen was going off to Ft Bragg, Jason went to his grandson's room, sat on the edge of the bed, and for a moment, watched Stephen pack his belongings. The US Army orders of items to bring to boot camp showing on Stephen's tablet was sitting on the bed adjacent to Jason. He picked up the tablet, glanced at the list, and said, "There are things on this list that you will appreciate when you don't have them. There will be plenty of times when you are out in the field. Stephen, please have a seat. I want to speak with you."

"Sure, Grandpa," he responded and sat down in his bedroom easy chair. Holding out the tablet in his hand, Jason spoke to his seventeen-year-old teenager.

"These orders are the very beginning of what the military is, just that, orders. Everything will be new and strange to you. The Drill Sergeants, DI's, will constantly order and direct you to perform every task required to become a ranger. You've already read about their physical conditioning program. It is very much more intense than any training you have ever done. It is designed to strain you, push you to the limits of your abilities, and deprive you of sleep and food to see how it messes with your mind. You are going to encounter many things you have never encountered before. You will experience this intense training for two years. I would never allow you to do this if I wasn't sure you were capable. I have already seen you working out, preparing for their physical test, knowing you can pass it. You are bright, smart, tough, physically fit, can run with speed and endurance, and you are solid as a rock. With the absolute newness and their methods of training, you will test your mental strength. You know you won't have Rachael and Suzanne's softness, guidance and kindness, Alicia's cooking and other services, no Coach Brown, and of course, you won't have the security and comforts of living at home. You have been protected and sheltered from the real world. You have always been able to make friends easily, and I suspect this will be no different. However, this special training will be intense and cause a lot of candidates to drop out along the way. Expect it! Make friends and help each other through. If you expect something and it happens, you are better prepared to deal with it. I also want to tell you something really important. If you decide to leave, don't make it, or really want out for whatever reason, there is no such thing as failing. Never, ever feel ashamed of attempting anything in your life. There are times in everyone's life when the universe lets us know that this may not be our best choice. Everyone is created with their own special talent. Sometimes when we are looking for *our calling,* that is to say, our reason for being here on earth, we search in many unfamiliar places and may do poorly. We are not here to do everything perfectly. As a matter of fact, Stephen, we are all perfectly imperfect! No matter what happens, you will learn purpose, discipline, mental strength, and courage. And if you go on choosing medical as your MOS specialty, you certainly will be highly educated in emergency medical treatment. Your football career will have to wait. Unfortunately, your football practices will cease, but I want you to consider throwing the football every chance you get and, if possible, play on any army football team you can. Your physical abilities will improve with the rangers, and you will probably lose some weight. That's okay. Watch very carefully what you eat. Obviously, I can no longer provide you with your nutritional supplements, but I will give you a list of foods, vitamins, and herbs you can add to your meals. And last, the most important. Up to now, I have made all the decisions concerning your life. I was in a position to be able to raise you the best way I believed I could. You have had a private tutor for your education, a private coach for your football and other sports, and special privileges no one else has received. You were brought up with good manners and taught to be respectful to everyone. As you know, I am extremely health conscious, especially about what goes inside your body. The things I chose for you, even forced upon you, I believe you will never regret. Now, today, I stand as a distant advisor, and it is you who will be at the helm making all of your own decisions; sometimes, you will make decisions that appear to be mistakes but are really a lesson that had to be learned. You will encounter an enemy that wants to kill you and all of America. Since birth, some of our enemies have been brainwashed to hate. They believe killing 'infidels' is good, and if they die doing it, they will be rewarded. To me, their beliefs come under the word 'ism'. They don't fight to protect their family or country. They fight to kill everyone who disagrees with their religion, including women and children, destroying everything in their path. Any 'ism' is difficult to destroy. You have to kill an 'ism' at its roots. Your missions in Special Ops will probably be related to finding those cowards hiding out who send out misguided children with bombs strapped to their bodies to commit suicide. Have no reservations about killing their leaders! The world will be a much better place without

144

them. Stephen, my grandson, we all love you and wish you the best. You will see things, hear things and have experiences you never imagined. You will be abruptly introduced to your manhood, and you will come back a different person!"

Chapter XXVII

As soon as he stepped off the bus, they were on him. "Whoa, big boy, what's your name, and how old are you?" yelled a Sergeant.

"Stephen Kellogg, I'm seventeen," he answered.

Stephen was now 6'6", 240 lbs. He had to duck when he came off the bus.

"Well, Kellogg, you think a kid with a big-sized body like you can make it through ranger school?"

"Yes," replied Stephen.

"Recruit, from now on; you will address me as Sergeant. Do you understand Kellogg?"

"Yes, Sergeant."

"Good, you look special, Kellogg; I want you put in my outfit. You'll love it, won't you, Kellogg?"

"Uh…" is all Stephen could think of to say.

"What?" yelled Sergeant Ansley tiptoeing to reach Stephen's ear, "I can't hear you, mister."

"Yes, Sergeant," Stephen yelled back.

"Now, you see those barracks over there?" the Sergeant asked as Stephen turned to look.

"Yes, Sergeant."

"You see that flag with a big letter C on it, Charlie Company?"

Again, Stephen answered, "Yes, Sergeant."

"Get your gear and butt over there on the double and see Sergeant Weller. You're mine, Kellogg. I'm going to eat you for breakfast. We'll see if you got what it takes to be a ranger, mister monster," yelled Sergeant Ansley again in Stephen's ear as he started to gather his gear and hustle toward the barracks. "I said on the double, recruit," he yelled again.

As soon as Stephen arrived at the barracks, he put his gear on the ground near the door entrance, slowly turned the handle until the door opened, and he peeked in. He looked to the right side of the barracks and saw other recruits settling in around their cots and emptying their belongings into huge foot chests while chatting with one another. He stepped back, picked up his baggage, and walked in. Again he had to duck under the door. As he entered, he turned his head to the right and asked if anyone could direct him to Sergeant Weller. A couple of guys pointed to an enclosed office on the left and said, "Over there!"

He walked up to the closed door and knocked twice, "Yes," replied a voice.

"Sergeant Ansley directed me to see Sergeant Weller."

"Well, come right in," was the reply with a very sarcastic tone. Leaving his baggage outside the office door, he opened the door to see a man with a broad, muscular build sitting behind a typical GI-issued desk.

He walked toward the Sergeant's desk, not knowing where to go or stand or even what to say, which made him anxious, so he leaned into the desk and blurted out, "Sergeant Weller, my name is Stephen Kellogg, and um…I was told to report to you for duty."

Dead silence. The Sergeant looked down at some report on his desk and didn't raise his head for a few minutes, but it felt like an hour to Stephen. Then, quickly and suddenly, he set the report aside and looked at Stephen dressed in civilian clothes and gave his new recruit a sly smile. He stood up and walked around the desk, and looked at Stephen. "You are a big fellow, aren't you; have you ever played football?"

"Yes, Sergeant."

"I thought so. You guys think that you can become a ranger because you play a game well. What's your name again?"

"Kellogg…Stephen Kellogg," the young boy replied.

"I'm going to save you a lot of aches and pains, Kellogg. Leave now. No one will blame you. Hey, you got to apply to be a ranger, right? That's a big step, cause look, what we have found out is that guys that are too big, can't run, can't keep up over the long haul, do you know what I mean, Kellogg?"

"Yes, Sergeant, I think so," Stephen said softly.

"Then why waste everyone's time? There's another bus leaving within the hour, you can go back to Sergeant Ansley, and he'll arrange for you to return home, then you can play some football. How's that sound?"

"It sounds like good advice for those who can't keep up, Sergeant, but it doesn't sound like me," Stephen replied.

"So am I hearing that you are staying here, recruit?"

"Yes, Sergeant, and if you would, I'd like to get my bunk assignment so I can unpack my things."

"Oh, you would, would you!" cried the Sargent in a much less friendly tone. "Well, first, Kellogg, we're going to teach you how to do everything the army way, and for now, mister, the army way is me!" tip-toeing up and yelling in Stephen's ear. "Is that clear, Kellogg?" again, increasing the volume of his words while edging closer to Stephen's ear.

"Yes, Sergeant, but honestly, Sergeant, you don't have to tip toe and yell in my ear. I can hear you perfectly."

In a much softer tone, Weller said: "Oh, is that right, Kellogg, you can hear perfectly; well, I'll just pass that along to Sergeant Ansley, and we'll all start our little quiet welcome program tomorrow morning, does that sound all right with you Kellogg?"

"Yes, Sergeant," replied the newly excited boy.

"Now, I want you to go out there with the other new recruits, introduce yourself and find a bed that's just right for you. And by the way, remind me tomorrow to teach you how to stand at attention, okay Kellogg?" the Sergeant said quietly.

"Yes, Sergeant," was the reply.

"Dismissed, Kellogg," were the last words before closing the office door, now with just a few hours left in his *old* world. Early, early tomorrow morning would be the beginning of his *new* world.

Before the next morning arrived, Stephen lay in his bunk all night, eyes wide open, facing straight up with his head resting on his hands, thinking about all the things he didn't know. His eyes became watery. He would never, however, let himself cry, *especially here.* For the very first time in his life, he felt alone, leaving him only with his thoughts. When a human anticipates something and has no idea of what to expect and has no previous experience, the mind's ego, which always wants to be in control, goes into fear because of uncertainty. To protect itself, it produces thoughts that build upon each other and, if not consciously stopped, will create a negative story because it was created from fear, not love. Stephen, young, innocent, and inexperienced in warfare, never before left to live in an unknown environment such as he was now in, was visiting all those thoughts of fear. Could he eat the food that was served, perform with sleep deprivation, was he mentally strong enough to make it, could he run the long haul, and could he ever kill another human being, were just some of the thoughts he had that night. But the biggest one of all was recalling his grandfather's last words: "You will come back a different person!"

"What did he mean?" Stephen wondered for a long while, trying to imagine what 'different' looked like. When he was able to accept a thought and then let it go, he was finally able to fall asleep.

Chapter XXVIII

The first weeks were total chaos for Stephen; classes, lectures, physical fitness training and tests, weapons training, running with full packs, always running, on and on, one day after the other, day after day, never stopping with little sleep. There was no time to be homesick. Stephen didn't have a chance to think about anything else. *Just follow directions and do what you are told!* As prepared as he thought he was, he learned he had no idea what he was getting into until the initial shock of reality set in. It scared him to think how much he would have to endure to become a ranger. But he committed to going with the flow and surviving every test and task, which he repeated to himself as he saw others dropping out. He decided he *had* to make it no matter what it took! He was so unfamiliar with army life. He had to make huge adjustments to his previous way of living. There were plenty of times when his superiors would make him look stupid because he was so young and so big. But he took it all and soon grew into the routine and slowly became a soldier. When he had a rare open moment, he would call or text Grandpa to always say hello and ask about his family, which now included young Jessica. He made many close friends in those early years as he gained tremendous respect from his instructors and fellow rangers. He went from being known as 'monster man' to 'the quarterback kid' because of his constant throwing of the football with anyone he could get to play catch. They all had seen what he could do throwing through hanging and swinging old truck tires used as targets and saw him as a little child always so eager to play football. He stayed a careful eater, eating healthier products and forgoing the rest. He would avoid certain foods altogether, even though he would go to bed hungrier than usual. That was okay. Better to have an empty stomach than one filled with chemicals and sugar, the stuff that made him feel sick. He ate only a minimum of processed foods. However, out in the field with individual rations, it was impossible to maintain his diet. When he ate out alone or with his fellow rangers, he would order the cleanest food he could find on the menu but couldn't possibly know exactly what was in it. And so, social eating, which is usually processed foods, was not the ideal platform for his health, and he knew it. He paid the price, upsetting his system and causing him to feel sick. He tried to keep up with the supplements his grandpa had recommended, but at this time in his life, some things were very much out of his control, so he did the best he could. Because of his ranger physical fitness program, he was still in great shape and gained minimum weight. He was very attractive to young ladies. He was always pleasant and respectful to the women he met. He liked women, but he was already in love, so just looking was fine for him. He felt he had a big challenge and

153

commitment ahead of him, and anything could happen along the way and believed he needed to focus on his goals with no further burdens, impediments, or baggage. His socializing with the opposite sex only showed how much more he loved Jess. After completing two years of training, Stephen was inducted into the rangers at the Ft. Bragg Rangers' Induction Ceremony. Stephen was able to get a three-day pass home to visit Jessica and his grandfather. On the last day of Stephen's leave, with just enough time to say hello, Jason invited all the family, along with Coach Brown and his family, Rachael and her family, Zachary Blankhardt and his family, and Julia Tressman, to come to the complex. Stephen wanted it that way, a short visit. There was no reason to mention anything about his training, experiences, or politics, just 'hello' and lots of love and good health messages passed around. It was his life, challenge, and commitment; it only mattered to him. He noticed how grown-up, pretty and cute Jessica was becoming, and it created an excitement in him he had never before experienced. When they were alone and conversing about what was happening in her life, he suddenly kissed her. "I couldn't help it, "he said. She gave him a big smile, kissed him back, and held him.

"I think I like you, Stephen H. Kellogg." They talked for a long while and promised each other that they would stay in contact every day by email and social media. Just then, Jason brought everyone together for a home-cooked meal by Alisa in honor of Stephen's visit home. After eating meals in the army and elsewhere, he now truly appreciated what it meant to eat healthy, delicious organic Alisa food. As he ate and chatted, he realized how fortunate he was to have been brought up in such a loving 'family' and with good friends, who were all such amazing people. He shared how much they meant to him when he raised his glass and said he was grateful to have them. He also told them how honored he was for the experience of working with a team of army specialists, even more efficient than a football team, because it was about life or death situations, not just a game. He returned to Bragg that night, thought about the visit, especially Jessica, and fell into a deep sleep.

Chapter XXIX

His missions would now begin. For the subsequent two years of active combat duty, Stephen was fortunate enough to be with teams that never lost a man. He will later recall the two pilots who died on his first mission as the only US casualties he experienced in service. As to his experiences of enemy death, he never knew if he killed anyone. In his mind, he was only there to accomplish his mission, and killing enemy soldiers would be the last means to get the job done because taking out a bad guy is still taking a human life. It's not just a paper target you shoot at. He used to wonder why the human species could kill their own kind so easily, while most other animals just fight it out for leadership or power but do not kill their opponent. He supposed that it was because man has the ability to think. "Remove the human brain from the body, and suddenly without thinking, we all live in the moment, in peace, without hate."

Stephen remembered once when his grandfather shouted out loud after being enraged by a hate crime. Stephen decided he would shoot to kill only when absolutely necessary. His heart did not change.

Stephen acquired some of his closest lifelong friends during his four years of active duty. He learned a long time ago from his grandfather to make friends 'wherever you are or go'. Now known as the 'Quarterback kid', all the rangers knew Stephen was special and would be a star in the pros. He practiced constantly, played on the local army football teams, and watched as many college and pro football games as time would allow. During this period, he met a new man, Beau Bellino, who was assigned to his ranger team. Beau had played football all his life and was a high school star receiver, almost as tall as Stephen but weighed much less. One day, early in their relationship, while dining together in the mess hall, Beau asked, "I don't see you eating much of anything except fruits, salads, and vegetables. How the hell did you get so big?"

"I was born that way, you know, like the Jolly Green Giant," smiled Stephen.

"Sure, and what the hell did he eat, growth hormones in his vegetables? Listen, kid, things change fast around here. Before you came here, I was known as *Monster Man* around this place; then, when they saw me practicing my throws all the time, they decided to call me the *Quarterback Kid*. It's all in prospective, soldier."

Stephen eventually told Beau about his young life with his grandpa being a nutritionist and growing up on a special nutritional formula, never eating processed or sugar-added foods, only drinking distilled water, and daily physical conditioning routines, mentioning the name Hercules as a workout buddy. When Beau asked who Hercules was, Stephen answered, "If you're lucky, someday I'll introduce you to him." They laughed together. Beau Bellino, from New Jersey, also wanted to serve his country before college or a career. He was fast, quick, and could catch. He and Stephen became the closest of friends and teammates. Together their pass completions and touchdowns on the local army team were incredible. Stephen spent most of his spare practice time honing his skills with Beau and knew how talented he was. And, of course, vice-versa. Beau was a year behind Stephen; thus, Stephen would attend college first and had hope of getting Beau to enroll at the same college the following year.

Stephen studied his medical manuals, ops plans, written training exercises, and anything pertaining to his job or mission during his meal times. He never stopped, so he had very little time to think about anything. He had so many commitments. He was always 'doing'. And when you are doing, your mind is focused, and you lose track of time. This made his four years of service go by fast. He kept all his special operation experiences to himself. It only mattered to the men involved. After being discharged from active duty at twenty-one years old, he entered the reserves and started studying for his college entrance exams.

Now, in many ways, a much different man than before he was a soldier. He would take charge of his own life and choose the paths he wanted to travel.

The biggest change of all was going from totally dependent to totally independent. He learned the meaning of leadership, trust, team member, and self-confidence. While traveling home, he recalled his grandfather's words at the last meeting before boot camp, "You will come back a different person." This time, he knew exactly what those words meant! Stephen knew his life had been sheltered but never imagined the outside world as he had just lived through as a soldier. He also realized that for seventeen years of his life, he never really questioned any of his life's decisions being made for him by his grandfather. He never thought he had a choice. He trusted and believed in his wisdom and all the persons who were hired on his behalf. He knew his grandfather was rich, and even though he had no mother or father, he was considered by other kids to be *born with a silver spoon in his mouth.* But to Stephen, that didn't mean life was easy and that there was no mental anguish or stress for him. There were a lot of times in his life that he felt embarrassed or ashamed of who he was because of his size or his *far-out* diet or his coach or nanny being around him all the time. He had to learn to swallow it, take that angry energy and transform it into something else, usually throwing footballs through a swinging tire, learning that tactic at a young age from Coach Brown. It was after Stephen told the coach about an incident during one game when he heard some of the boys on the other team saying things about him that he could hear. That's what made Coach Brown so good. It wasn't that he could teach football to kids, but it was how he could relate to his students and use examples in life, stressing a take-charge attitude toward anger. "Allow the anger. It's natural, then convert it for your good use," he would say. Coach Brown *was* his 'father'.

Chapter XXX

After his discharge from active duty, Stephen was eager for his new life to begin. He made his way home on his own without telling anyone he was coming. After surprising Alicia at the door with a big bear hug and then poking his head into Jason's office to surprise Rachael, Suzanne, and his grandfather, with three more hugs, Stephen then visited his second family, his lifelong friends, Hercules, Venus, and now their two new baby chimps. When he returned to the house, everyone sat down for dinner, and when it was over and everyone had left, Jason motioned to Stephen, and the two men started walking toward the library. Stephen settled in and sat down beside his grandfather on the same exact couch where another serious conversation had taken place four years ago, the day before Stephen's departure to ranger boot camp. After settling in, Jason spoke. "First of all, even though we have visited and kept up with each other over these four years, we have never spoken about your military life or many other important matters. I want to tell you how grateful I am that you are safe, and right this moment, I am being egotistically proud of what *you* have accomplished," as he put his arm around his grandson's huge shoulder. "I want to listen to anything you would like to share with me, with the understanding that for whatever reasons, we will only discuss topics that you wish to discuss. I can see with

161

my own eyes how well you look physically, and from what I understand, you have gotten and will still do a lot of testing and receive counseling support from the army to be sure there are no mental issues associated with what you have seen and done during your training and combat missions. You are your own man now, but no one is ever too big or too small to seek help on any issue. I am, and will always be, here for you."

Stephen smiled at his grandfather. "Let's talk tomorrow, Grandpa. It has been a wonderful but long day."

The following morning after breakfast, Stephen found Jason working in his office. He knocked on the door and said, "May I come in, Grandpa?"

"Of course, please sit down, and I'll finish this project so we can talk." After a few moments, Jason spoke. "Well, Stephen, did you enjoy your civilian breakfast from Alicia this morning?"

"You know, Grandpa, I realize now how spoiled I am to have been lucky enough to be your grandson and have such a great cook. I sure wish I could have taken her along with me. Eating the right foods while I was in the service was a big challenge. But I guess I made it through, and now I can properly care for myself the way I want. So no harm done, Grandpa. When I had to do my own shopping, boy did I notice how much sugar there is in everything. No wonder there is so much obesity and sickness in this country. Do people not really care what they put in their body, or are manufacturers steering them in the sugar direction and they are not aware?"

"I wish I knew," replied Jason.

"It is amazing how better people feel after reducing their sugar intake and losing weight. How do we explain this to our fellow citizens to get a healthier country? Maybe someday we will be able to, Grandpa," Stephen said. Then he changed the subject.

"Grandpa, last night you mentioned that we will only talk about the topics I wish to speak of, and I appreciate that very much. I obviously couldn't mention anything about my training or missions in my communications to you, but I am sure you were aware of what was going on through the news and social media. I did want to discuss my first mission, which was unsuccessful because we never reached our destination. It was my first encounter with death. Our two pilots died, and the rest of the team sustained injuries when our helicopter crashed. Everyone had a debilitating injury, a broken bone, a sprained ankle or knee, and I had only received minor bruises and little pain. It took a while to get over the actual deaths of our own servicemen, and I almost felt responsible because, as their medic, I never had a chance to save them. I cried that night, Grandpa. But that's not the reason I am bringing up this incident. How was I able to remain whole? I mean, I ask myself, how was I able to stay uninjured? I bounced around the chopper like everyone else, yet I came out with just scratches."

After listening to Stephen's story, Jason replied, "There was probably an element of luck. But don't you remember a while back when the Patriots had quarterback Tom Brady who had a very restricted diet, never eating processed sugar or white flour? He very rarely got injured. I had put you on a similarly strict diet of healthy foods and added other ingredients that were designed to build a stronger body, which also may have helped you stay uninjured. You certainly know how strong and fast you are playing football and making it to the top of your class in ranger school. Because of how you started off in life, living with a dedicated nutritionist as I am, you are probably one of the strongest men and most highly educated, I might add, in the country, if not the world."

Stephen thought for a while. "All these years, Grandpa, and this is the first time I have ever spoken to you about who I am, or maybe what I am, and why." In a calm inquisitive tone, Stephen continued, "Why did you do all of this, Grandpa? I have only known you to devote your whole life to me. You could have easily remarried twenty years ago and started a new family. Why did you build such a complex, hire tutors and a football coach, and keep me on your special diet?"

As Stephen was looking for a response from his grandfather, who was still searching for words, there was a moment of unsure silence in the room. Something felt heavy and weighing on both men. It was their inner vibrations of tension each one was feeling. Jason turned and walked to the window, stopped, and looked out. After a while, he turned around and faced Stephen. "Well, you are at that age in life when you are entitled to know, and I knew I would have to tell you someday." Jason then, from his point of view, told Stephen about the dreams of his grandmother, Jean, and decided to use his nutritional knowledge to raise this 'child spared by the Creator', with a healthy lifestyle, exceptional education, and play football as a stepping stone to his destiny," Jason said. "I intended that with your powerful body, your many languages, knowledge and capabilities on the football field, along with a superior education, someday you could take all you have learned and do something amazingly good for the world…*something*, Stephen, that would better mankind! I don't know what that *something* will be, but I do know in my heart that I have given you the tools for that success." There was a pause, then Jason continued. "After everyone passed away, I had no one in my life but you. I loved and missed them all, and I knew that if I didn't bury myself in my work, I could have gone into depression or worse. So after the dreams, I decided to willingly devote my life to you and guide you through your young life until you left to become a ranger. I wanted you to learn all about George Washington because I selfishly feel his virtues, ideals, character, stature, and leadership best represent what America can be without this political extremism, disgusting and disgraceful political advertising, and racial hate. You have read, listened, and learned everything about George Washington, the first man to follow the constitution and walk away from being king and all that power! I wanted you to be able to speak many languages so you could better communicate with the rest of the world. I also wanted you to build character while serving your country with the army rangers as George Washington served his new country with men willing to die for their freedom. So here you are in front of me, my grandson, my only tie to Jean, your grandmother, your mother, my daughter," he said softly, "and your father, my son-in-law. Did I have a right to do what I have done? I don't know, Stephen. I know that what I have done is for *my* right reasons, but I don't know if I had the right to steer and mold your life as I did. You had led an extremely sheltered life before the army. I knew your service would change all that and let you take control of your life now. I will forever support you in all your decisions and give you my counsel whenever requested. Frankly, I feel relieved. I feel inspired to look to the future of watching you grow on whatever path you decide. I love you and have tried to be the best grandfather I could be, feeling that you were saved for some special reason, and I was to play my part."

Stephen paused, "I don't know what to say right now, Grandpa. I need some time to understand all this. I'd like to talk about the dreams you had about grandma Jean." It was then that Jason noticed that he was sweating.

Stephen had been listening intently. He realized he was no longer a young, innocent boy. For a moment, his mind turned to Hercules and the chimpanzee's amazing size and strength and realized how he, Stephen, had also become so big and strong. He felt an eerie tingle in his body as he recognized this connection to Hercules. He had to let his grandfather's explanations linger in his mind before deciding what to do next. Then Stephen got up from his seat, went over to his grandpa, hugged and kissed him, and said: "Well, now it's my turn, Grandpa, and I will always want your advice. Right now, I just want to finally see Jess, go to college, and play football."

"Stephen," replied Jason, who smiled as he spoke, "you have earned it. I have set aside a college fund for you if you need it."

"Don't need it, Grandpa; your days of supporting me are over. Along with my military schooling benefits, savings, and a potential football scholarship, I will be able to attend college."

"Do you have any plans yet on what college you would like to attend?" asked Jason.

"I know I want to be close to Jessica," replied Stephen.

"I'm sure you can find a college close by. You and Jess have been in close communication these past years. Is there anything I should know? Not yet, but it's no secret that I do like her a lot!"

They spent the better part of the evening interpreting Jason's dreams, and when the evening ended, both men felt complete, and calmness settled upon them.

After the 'remarkable' tale Stephen heard from his grandfather and future plans they subsequently discussed, he could barely sleep that night. Stephen still didn't know what that *something* would be and had a lot of thoughts about it, but both had agreed that the day would come when Stephen *would know*. He knew he needed time to tie all the pieces together. He sat up in the darkness, put the pillow against the headboard, and rested his head on it just as he had done on the first day of army ranger school. He closed his eyes and drove his memory back as far as he could remember, first remembering the tiny footballs hanging above his crib and then first learning to throw a football with his grandfather. After being told the story about his parents and grandmother's deaths, he remembered how he cried after Rachael brought him to an orphanage to visit other children who also had no parents and how he hugged Rachael so tight that day. Then he thought about Jessica and fell asleep with that sweet vision still inside his head. The next morning, he let his grandpa know how eager he was to visit Jessica and that the first thing he wanted to do was to fly to New England and visit Jess, who was now seventeen and headed to undergraduate school. They had kept their promise to stay in touch as Stephen was enamored with her. It was now time to select colleges, and he was eager to see her, to say the least!

Part Eight: The Formidable Years

Chapter XXXI

Jason got up from his seat, extended his hand to Zachary across the restaurant table, and said, "Zack, wasn't that some game today?"

It was Stephen's junior year at Harvard; they had just won their last game of the season and were undefeated. Zack was beaming and said, "It was that last touchdown run by Stephen that nailed it. What a great game he played. He deserves to win the Heisman Trophy. We should be ranked number one in the nation," he replied to Jason. The remaining entourage from the stadium box were now entering a fine dining Boston restaurant and heading into a private room for dinner while awaiting Stephen and Jessica to arrive. The room was filled with close friends. There was Zack and his wife, two of his married children along with spouses and grandchildren, Rachael, her husband and Jessica's younger sister, Rachael's previous assistant Suzanne, and her husband, Coach Brown and his wife, and Mrs. Tressman, who was now, Mrs. Julia Davies. There was excitement in the air. Everybody was smiling and chatting about the game and Stephen's accomplishments. This was not the first time Jason and Zack had been to a game together. As a matter of fact, Senator Zachary Blankhardt, a former graduate of Harvard University, had the use of corporate box seats any time he wanted to see a game in a booth overlooking the field at the top of the stadium. And ever since Stephen started playing football at Harvard three years ago, Zack and Jason were together for all the games. Both now in their seventies, they had remained very close friends over the years, and to Stephen, Zack was always 'Uncle Zack'. Zack had always been close to Stephen and watched him grow, train, and be tutored, all in an uncommon fashion, and it fascinated Zack to follow Stephen's life. He marveled at Stephen's ability on the field and even earlier in life when he played with the chimpanzees. Zack would watch how Stephen learned to jump and swing with stealthy speed. So when the time came, he was extremely happy to offer his name as a reference on Stephen's Harvard application. Stephen had come to Uncle Zack on at least two prior occasions, one for counsel on his military service and the other while deciding between West Point and Harvard. That's when Stephen decided that as much as he loved and admired George Washington, a military career was not his desire, and thus he chose Harvard as his first choice. Next year, he would complete his army reserve obligation's final year and become retired military. However, all of his close friends he served with in the army rangers would always be his close lifelong friends because they never would forget what they went through together; no matter what color, religion, or race, they were lifelong 'brothers'.

And Jason had followed Zachary's political career ever since they met so many years ago when the 'project' began. But after Jason lost his family, Zack knew that Jason had only one thing on his mind. Jason's obsession with his dreams of Jean were his beliefs and thus became his reality. His life centered on the phrase: "From all the loss, sadness, and darkness cast upon my life from the loss of my family, I will rise from the ashes like a phoenix and do all that I can to bring goodness and joy in the world through my grandson." Zack was no stranger to Jason's goal of Stephen *doing something great, or something magnificent*. Zack, Stephen, and 'family' were the only ones who ever heard Jason use that phrase. But Zack really didn't yet know exactly what that phrase meant. Up to now, no one knew. For all Zack knew, it could have referred to football statistics, trophies, anything. Right this moment, however, Zack couldn't get over the fact that Harvard still had a chance to be ranked the number 1 football team in all of America! And, Stephen H. Kellogg, his 'nephew', was the reason.

Stephen and Jessica soon arrived, and everyone in the restaurant cheered and clapped as they walked through the lobby toward the private room as if to notify the occupants in the dining room that their guests had arrived. Again as the door opened, there were generous greetings and compliments to Stephen, who, by now, was accustomed to large groups of fans, TV commentators, and crowded rooms. He took all the words gracefully and warmly as he met his guests' eyes. After all the greetings and pleasantries were exchanged, the room settled down, and dinner was served. Jessica was now twenty-one years of age and graduating from undergraduate school. She had already been accepted to Harvard Law School, majoring in International Law and Relations. While Stephen wasn't quite sure of his next move because of his eligibility for the NFL draft, he knew he wanted to stay in Boston to be with Jessica. So while dessert was being served, Stephen rose from his seat, asking for quiet as he had an announcement. "My dear family and friends, I have fallen deeply in love with this young woman," staring down into Jessica's eyes with the biggest smile, "And tonight, we are excited to inform you that we are engaged to soon be married," as he held out her hand to show her modest engagement ring. For Stephen, that's when the real celebration started.

Three years before, while Stephen was determining which school would be best for him, he had Coach Brown do some searching around for him.

"I started with the schools you were most interested in, Harvard and West Point. However, neither needed a quarterback this year. Then I checked out the big schools. There were openings, but I'll leave you the pros and cons for you to review. I know there are more reasons to pick a school

174

besides football. So let me know when you are ready to discuss the subject." Stephen listened intently to Coach Brown.

"Coach, no time like the present," replied Stephen. He looked at the list of schools the coach had given him and, after a few minutes, said, "Your notes here under Harvard say that the quarterback is a senior, and next year, there will be tryouts for a new one. Is that correct?"

"Yes, West Point is the same situation," replied Brown.

"Harvard has the courses I want to study, and I could be close to Jessica. Do you think the Harvard coach would let me try out this year for fullback or running back and let me play both sides of the ball at linebacker, too?" asked Stephen.

"That's a tall order, Stephen, but I'll speak to him."

"Thanks, coach."

"When did you start playing football?" Coach O'Brien asked Stephen. Having passed all his exams and requirements to be accepted to Harvard, notwithstanding being the 'nephew' of Senator Zachary Blankhardt, Stephen was excited and enthusiastic when speaking to the Harvard coach.

"I think I was born with a football in both hands," replied Stephen with a full smile on his face.

The coach looked up from his desk, smiled back, and said, "Coach Brown has asked me to give you a tryout with our team. He has informed me that you want to play quarterback, and of course, as you now know, our new senior quarterback has been training and waiting to play that position for a long time, and I am obliged to start him. However, you would be eligible to compete for that position next year or, of course, be eligible in the event of an injury this year. Coach Brown also informed me that after speaking with you concerning the quarterback matter, you would be interested in trying out for a running back position and a linebacker, playing both sides of the football in the same game. That's the most unusual request I have ever received. Now that I see your size and condition, I can understand why you might be good at both positions. Frankly, I don't know if it can be done, but I am willing to be open to it. But first, tell me, why did you select this school?"

"There are a few reasons I selected Harvard," Stephen explained. "First and foremost is that this school has the best courses I am majoring in, and I want the education, not just playing football. Second, my girlfriend goes to school in this state close by this school. And third, I have an army reserve duty to complete while I am in school, and the reserve armory is right nearby. The school is allowing me to take classes online, allowing me to practice with the team, and at the same time, doesn't interfere with my reserve obligations. Coach Brown and I have discussed and looked at all the possibilities, and I am willing to wait and compete for those positions this year. But I must confess, I am really eager to play football at any position, just so I can play. I am four years older than the average college freshman, so my future years to play are shortened. I want to play as soon as possible, and Coach Brown said you were looking for a running back this year, and I am ready for the challenge for the chance to play quarterback next year."

"Well, that makes sense, Stephen. Let's see you out with the team on the field starting tomorrow morning at 8:00 AM. If you are as good as Coach Brown thinks, we will find you a place on the team." Coach O'Brien got up from his chair and extended his arm across the desk as Stephen rose to shake his hand.

"See you in the morning, coach," was Stephen's enthusiastic reply.

By mid-morning, the offensive coach walked over to Coach O'Brien and whispered, "Where did this Kellogg kid come from?" he asked.

"Well, he spent four years in the Army Special Forces before coming here and played football for the army, and before that, he went to Russell Prep. According to our Hall of Fame Coach, George Brown, who has been the kid's coach since five years old, Kellogg can play *any* position well enough to make *any* team. He chose us because his girlfriend is at school close by," replied O'Brien.

"The defense can't stop him," replied the offensive coach, "I have never seen a more conditioned player with such strength and agility. This guy is something!"

With the first official opening game coming up, Stephen felt comfortable within the team. The preseason games had finished, and while playing running back, Stephen had scored many of the teams' touchdowns, displaying his abilities to his teammates and opponents. Stephen's first year at running back earned him a first position on the College All-America Team and honorable mention for a defensive linebacker, never before accomplished by anyone in college football. He set school records. His coaches and teammates became fully respectful of his remarkable ability to play any position impeccably. At one practice, when O'Brien asked Stephen if he ever kicked a field goal, Stephen replied by kicking a 60-yard field goal right through the center of the goal posts. The coach's mouth stayed wide open for a few seconds, then he said, "What am I going to do with you, Kellogg? You can't play every position at the same time!"

By the end of the preseason, the players and staff began to recognize the prospect that Harvard could actually win a lot of football games. And they did! Their first game was away at nearby Dartmouth. Jessica came to that game and, from then on, came to every game. And Stephen loved having her there because they could always spend a few precious moments alone after the games.

Chapter XXXIV

"Stephen, Uncle Zack and I are meeting here today before your new contract is to be negotiated, because we would like to propose something to you." In Jason's familiar rosewood library/office room the three men sat in tall back cushy leather chairs pulled close to form a small circle so they could face one another. Looking directly into Stephen's eyes, Zack started. "You know Stephen, your grandfather has told the story of your family, and in doing so, he has revealed to me that he has prepared you for something," he paused, "...something wonderful that will somehow help make a better world. And though he had mentioned this so-called plan of his to me, it was never really known how that would manifest itself into an opportunity to make this county and the world a better place.

Your grandfather has been a close friend and a big supporter of mine, having similar views, beliefs, and values, and we have always confided in each other over the years. As you know, when I retired many years ago to help my son Desmond with his campaign, I noticed how the division in the two parties was becoming deeper, with more and more money thrown at disgusting negative political ads, and, out and out lies being broadcast all over TV and social media." Stephen listened intently as he detected some anger from Zack that he had never felt before. "Eventually, as you know,

Chapter XXXII

When Stephen first started thinking about his college education, he wasn't at all sure of his major. He was highly educated overall, especially in foreign languages, and learned an awful lot about nutrition from his grandpa. He probably could do most anything, but he was still uncommitted. "l want to get deeper into American History and Constitutional Law, and maybe some courses in International Relations, American and foreign politics and later take a course in world religions. Then after experiencing freshman courses and college life, I'll hone in on what I would like to do the rest of my life after football," he thought to himself.

American History was what Stephen had come to love. There was no other country like America. Its foundations were unique at the time in history when kings, despots, and tyrants were ruling the world. Throughout his youth, Stephen had been led by Grandpa to learn all about George Washington, the father of our country. When Stephen was at a very young age, not yet able to read, Grandpa would read to him. And later on, after he learned to read and use audiobooks, which he listened to every day during his morning run, he would go deeper into the character of George Washington and the American patriot soldiers of the revolutionary war who stayed in the army through hell and high water because their freedom was everything; as opposed to some colony, so-called, 'sunshine soldiers', who were patriotic to whichever army was winning. He learned through his reading and education that 'radicals' can initiate world change, sometimes for good reasons and sometimes for not-so-good reasons. He was taught that a radical is someone who wants extreme change, usually with no compromises. Feeling stuck, imprisoned, and controlled, a few daring colonists became radicals in search of their freedom. They had mostly left Europe for that reason. Later on in life, when Stephen was older, in his teens, and pondering Grandpa's suggestion of military service, he recalled the battle of Trenton. He would ask himself: "How far would I go to fight for the love of freedom? How many losing battles does it take before I would run in fear? How did they do it? The frozen citizen-soldiers who stayed with Washington that Christmas were given the password 'Victory or Death', as they crossed Delaware to surprise the Hessians. They knew it would be a struggle just to get there, fighting for life or death, and they still went along. Could I have been one of them? Would I run? What is it that keeps one man going forward while another man runs? What does that say about their character?" he asked himself. He realized that the word was not easy to define because there were many meanings. He discovered that a person's character might not be seen except for possible physical signs in how one carries themselves, speaks, or reacts. But mainly, he learned through life that character is acquired over a long period of time through a collection of experiences. Every person's life experiences determine their character and confidence. Where do one's beliefs come from? The people who are part of a child's early life development greatly influence their behavior patterns that help determine their character. These everyday repetitive patterns, mostly unnoticed, have a tremendous effect on a child's future life. A grown person may not even know why they feel anxious, guilt, or shame. If a child has been drilled over and over to feel shame for his actions, then later on in life, that learned pattern of shame will automatically appear. The same is true for teaching love! Humans will unconsciously follow the patterns that have been systematically taught to them over and over again. Amazingly though, there are no two humans exactly alike. Our Creator chose to give every single human being their own fingerprint, as well as their own life story. A person's character is built daily through human interactions, choices, and thoughts that can easily turn into beliefs. And ultimately, beliefs become a huge part of how a person experiences life.

Stephen had grown up as a child playing with chimpanzees, which brought him a love and respect for animals and nature. He had accumulated an amazing 'one-on one' education and could speak and understand seven different languages. He had a visible quiet confidence in himself. He learned to keep his emotions under control because he was brought up accustomed to disciplined schedules of classes, football practice, studying, and eating habits which allowed him to make it through the discipline required at ranger school. And he surprised himself and boosted his confidence when he discovered that he dared to follow through on his training and his missions. He usually never answered a question quickly. He would hesitate a few seconds to think. He was always bigger and stronger than his peers but never abused his strength or size against anyone on the football field, in the army (except, of course, the enemy), or, for that matter, in life. However, most of his life before the military was always under protection by the mere isolation from the *real-life* outside Grandpa's estate. He experienced moments of fear mostly of the unknown, a normal human fear of imagining future events with negative thoughts, such as doing something for the first time and fearing failure. When he went on dangerous missions, what he felt wasn't all for himself; it was also fear of losing or injuring any member of his team. Armed with his positive and respectful views toward life and nature, his physical abilities, and his privately tutored education, up to this point in time, Stephen's *character* could be judged as impeccable. As he became a famous college football star, noted NFL great, and met lots of new people, he would also be considered a gentle, positive, respectful man with a friendly smile and a good heart.

Right after Jessica graduated, she learned she had been accepted to Harvard Law School. At almost the same time, Stephen was selected as the number one pick by the New England Patriots after only his third year at Harvard when he became eligible for the NFL draft. He gladly accepted because he wanted to stay in Boston. Both were excited about their new positions in life, and their celebration culminated with their wedding at Jason's house that summer. They honeymooned on a quiet island in Tahiti and found a house near Boston, halfway between Harvard and the Patriots' stadium, upon return. Stephen would continue his online undergraduate classes for another year to graduate from Harvard and complete his final year of army reserves while an NFL rookie. He was really happy to stay in Boston, which he loved because of its revolutionary history. After all, this is where freedom's call started! And so, when he learned that the Patriots were looking for a quarterback, he decided to be eligible for the draft. He knew he might not play the first year, but that was the case with any professional team. He felt his whole life up to now was to prepare him to play NFL football. This was it for Stephen, a lifetime goal of actually playing big-time football!

Now recognized almost everywhere he went in the Boston area; he couldn't go anywhere local without being stopped and having his autograph requested. And although he was always friendly and kind when it happened, he limited his time in public because he always had a busy schedule and cherished his privacy. At first, when he went out with Jess, she wasn't used to the attention, and she would politely go on her way visiting stores while he was engaged with some fans and would meet up afterward. As time went on, she realized that Stephen's life was always going to be filled with those moments, and she knew that their privacy would have to be a priority in their lives together. The great thing about their marriage was that they could communicate. And they did from the very first potential problem.

"I'll be away sometimes, and you may not be able to come to some games," explained Stephen. "I also realize that there will always be certain temptations around football players, which could create problems for them and their wives. I believe our marriage has been built on trust and love, and us even talking about things, no matter what it is, brings us closer to each other. I love that we can communicate. I will always honor and respect our trust for each other."

Jessica beamed after Stephen spoke those words. "I know I married a good man. I'm glad we can share our thoughts. Talking about certain matters before they occur avoids later conflicts. I totally agree. I truly believe that the more communication we have, the better our marriage."

And as time passed, those words proved to be ever so true.

Jessica's upbringing, education, and private life had been very similar to Stephen's. She was educated mostly by her mother and Suzanne. She had access to all of the compound's facilities and became a first-class swimmer like her mother. Growing up on Jason's compound, she became a background fixture being unnoticed around the football field. She would watch Stephen and the other players practice, and just by watching and listening, she learned football strategy so that over time she was no stranger to the game. Jessica, too, could speak many different languages, and she knew that after graduating from law school, she wanted to specialize in International Law with a firm in Boston. While in undergraduate school, she was an all-American swimmer and won a silver medal for the United States in the Summer Olympics. She didn't date while Stephen was in the army but would go out and socialize with her girlfriends and boyfriends. All they knew about Jessica's love life was when she casually mentioned that she had a boyfriend she liked who was in the army. She never said his name nor showed his picture. Neither did she admit that she had already fallen in love with him!

Both Stephen and Jessica were still young in the world. They had lived sheltered lives, and human struggle experiences and conflicts were very rare to them. Their early lives were easily controlled while being home schooled, having very few personal life experiences due to the lack of interaction with their peers. Life is much different when a kid wakes up and goes off to school somewhere where there are a lot of teachers and students as opposed to an isolated home-schooled student. It's almost like saying that up to the age of seventeen, they both were in denial of the world's human pain of everyday life simply because they never had much opportunity to experience such pain. Therefore their outlook on life had to be different from a child coming from a middle-class or low-income family whose kids had to attend local public schools for their education. They both knew they had been brought up differently than other normal kids, but they didn't know that every human being would someday have to face conflict and pain and learn how to handle it on their own terms. Like the real world, Stephen would have negative encounters because of one thing or another, but nothing compared to what would come later in his life.

Chapter XXXIII

After being the number one college football player of the year in his junior year at Harvard and receiving the prestigious Heisman Trophy that same year, The Patriots offered Stephen a multi-million dollar contract for five years. He asked Jason and Uncle Zack to be his contract negotiators with the Patriots. They gladly accepted and wisely advised him. The contract was a record-high salary, and Stephen knew he had to live up to it. Excited to play, Stephen went to his first summer football camp with the Patriots. He went through the introduction formalities with the staff, coaches, and players. He was assigned his locker right next to a fantastic receiver for the Patriots, Paul Botts, who was already a star-wide receiver. They would become very close friends. The first day was more or less orientation and meeting the team members. What a difference from college football. These players were mostly married with families and serious about playing football and being big-sized and proficient. Stephen noticed the high caliber of training and experience all the players had, and as good as he was, he knew there were many more things he needed to learn. But Stephen made friends easily, as always, and by the end of summer camp, he became friends with everyone on the team and knew their capabilities. He would start as the third-string quarterback, but by the end of camp and the beginning of preseason, he became the second-string quarterback, next in line to take over the position in the event of a trade, injury, or poor performance by the starting quarterback. Stephen was always ready to go on the field to play.

It was during the third regular-season game that Stephen had his chance. Quarterback Mike Bowers got injured late in the fourth quarter against the visiting Ravens and had to be assisted off the field. It was near the end of the game and would allow Stephen only a few minutes left, which turned out to be a blessing. The small amount of time left before the clock ran out allowed Stephen to experience the initial nervousness of being on the field for the first time as a professional athlete. Initially told and trained not to run, Stephen merely handed off the ball to the backs for three downs. Compared to college, after a few games, Coach O'Brien had let Stephen make his own decisions about what plays to call and allowed him to run on his own when necessary. The fans in the stands were excited to see their rookie Boston quarterback play, and luckily for the Patriots, they were able to squeeze a win by a last-second field goal ending the game. The New England fans cheered frantically, and the morning sports headlines mentioned the name Kellogg for the first time. The field goal kicker became the hero that day, and Stephen was happy just to be on the winning side of his first NFL game. Someone from

Stephen's past, now a seasoned, successful sportscaster at the leading sports network, Mike Glen, saw the name Stephen Kellogg come across the news wire, and his eyes lit up!

The first-string quarterback was out for the season. The Patriots played Stephen as their number one quarterback from that time on for the full length of his five-year contract. During that time, Stephen Kellogg became a household name across the nation. Not only did they let him call the plays in the huddle, but they also allowed him to run in a game that proved to be monumental. His running game was so strong that at one point, they were tempted to make him into a running back but quickly buried that idea because he was the only two-handed (left & right) passer in NFL history and was leading in all of the passing categories. During his second year with the team, Stephen contacted his close friend Beau Bellino, his fantastic receiver on the army team, to try out for the Patriots. Stephen put in a good word for him, and after being picked up by the Pats, both men had record-breaking seasons together. At the conclusion of his five-year contract, the Patriots had gone to the playoffs every year and won two Super Bowls with Stephen as MVP in both games. The Patriots eagerly wanted to sign Stephen for another contract. Once again, Jason and Zack assisted Stephen in negotiating a contract for eight more years at a big salary plus bonuses, and that period of time was just right for two advisors. Now with his salary, bonuses, and product endorsements, Stephen became a multi-millionaire in his own right.

While Stephen was becoming a football legend, Jessica secured her status as a specialist in international law, working for a top-notch firm in Boston. During that time, both worked continuously, and their time together became less and less as each grew more and more in their professions. With all the commitments professional football required, continuous interviews and guest speaking, product endorsements, social causes, and a fan club with millions of followers for Stephen, overseas flights, and late-night legal meetings for Jessica, it was a wonder that they had time to have children. But they did, a boy and a girl. Jessica took a leave of absence both times, and Grandma Rachael was there to help with the newborns. Grandpa Davies, now in his middle seventies and still in great health, was very excited to become a great-grandpa. However, on the sad side of life, Coach Brown passed away during Stephen's seventh year of playing professional football. Stephen and Jessica took it very hard and while giving his eulogy, Stephen referred to him 'as the closest thing I ever had for a father'. After the final season of Stephen's contract, just before new negotiations began, Jason and Zachary suggested meeting with Stephen for a talk.

Part Nine: Completing the Plan

Stephen, Desmond too, left politics because he saw the moderates on both sides losing voice to the extremists. Over time the clouds became darker, and then came the attack on the Capital. That was the last straw, my turning point. It shocked me! It's time America wakes up! It needs something else. And since that time, basically, nothing has changed. I began to think about why Americans are letting the extremes divide the country. Why are we allowing extreme views to rule our thinking? That's when I decided to seek the help of my dear old friend Jason to get his feelings on the subject. Stephen, I have been associated with politics all my life, and I am no angel. But I consider myself a decent and rational man. I have political beliefs as every American, but I did things in good faith. I voted for bills in Congress based on what would be best for the people of this country, for most Americans, knowing no bill will ever please everyone, but that's where negotiating begins, and that's what I was elected to do. But that's not happening anymore, and it hasn't happened in years and years because the extremes in each party are exploiting the American voters using old and many more new types of media to spread lies and twisted words, anything to win." There was a noticeable quiet pause, and then Zack said, "I'm going to give the floor to your grandfather now, who will further explain." Stephen said nothing and then took a sip of water.

"Uncle Zack has explained his views on our country's current political situation quite candidly, and I must admit that my views are not too dissimilar. I have only supported Zachary in donations and advice and never got involved in politics. I make those donations based on the man, the person, not the party. I have followed Zack throughout his career and believe he is an honest man with good intentions. He left his party because he lost faith in it. I can see why. For years now, Zack and I have been meeting about all these issues. I'll get right to it, Stephen; this country needs a third political party! A strong enough third party will counter the extremes. Right now, when one party gets in power, all the bills passed are mostly lopsided toward their extremist's view, and then when the other side gets in, the pendulum swings to the exact opposite extreme side and so on. But, if you don't have enough votes in your own party to pass a bill, negotiation with the third party is the only way to get the necessary votes, meaning concessions have to be given. Extremists do not like to give anything! They thrive when they can steer the party's view. Negotiating, giving something up, swipes their power away and brings all sides closer, as opposed to more divided. Bills get passed and will benefit many more people than just half the nation. Business gets done in the nation's capital. With a third party, I believe that a much, much larger percent of the people will rule the country, not a minutia of political extremists. You see, a third party can be a wedge on either side of the aisle. It's almost like having our political system with the same checks and balances as our own government! It will attract moderate, reasonable voters and act in the country's best interests, NOT THE PARTY!" There was a pause. "Stephen, we want YOU to run for President on a new third party in the next election two years from now." Stephen looked at Zack and then Jason, and then there was a smile on his face just before he started laughing and laughing and more laughing. And before he could say anything, Jason said calmly. "We really didn't know what reaction to expect, but I think laughing hysterically was not on the list." Everyone smiled for a moment, and Jason went on. "But before you ask the obvious and not so obvious questions, let me further explain that you have probably concluded by now that we have put a lot of thought into starting an organization of this magnitude, and we have. We have been talking about this moment for some time. It is necessary to bring this request at this time because we know your new contract is coming up shortly, requiring you to make a decision in about two weeks. If you decide to run, we will need these next two years to get organized. That means after playing thirteen years, you would have to leave professional football. It will be an astonishing announcement. Of course, you do not have to do this. This has to be your decision without regard to us. I, of all people in your life, would never ask you to leave football unless there was something more important, as was your military service. We definitely do not want a response today. But after you take time to think it through and discuss it with Jess, the answer must be from your heart. We will gratefully accept your decision either way." Stephen got up from the chair, walked toward the wide window, stood there, and unconsciously put his left hand on the back of his neck while looking out the window. Rubbing his neck and slowly sliding his hand back down his side, he turned around, faced them with a serious face, and said, "You both have been working on this for a very long time, haven't you?" They both nodded. "And you both think I can lead this country?" Jason answered. "Eight years as a trained medic in the rangers, two years as a ranger team leader, Silver Star recipient, four years as an instructor in the reserves, three-time college All-American, graduated Harvard near the top of his class, Heisman Trophy winner, first draft pick for the Patriots, five Superbowl wins and five times chosen as Superbowl MVP."

It was then that Zack chimed in. "As I understand it, at Harvard, you majored in American history, took religion courses, political courses, philosophy, and international politics. You speak fluently in many languages and are a mentor for many kids."

Jason jumped back in. "Oh, you can lead alright, Stephen." He paused a moment, picked up his arm, and with his index finger bent pointing toward Stephen, he said, "People admire you. They like you!"

Stephen responded. "You're giving me a whole two weeks to make this decision?" They both nodded and smiled. "I will meet you back here in one week, not with a decision, but with questions and thoughts." They both shook their heads in agreement.

Stephen got up, shook hands with Uncle Zack, and turned to face his grandpa to shake his hand when Jason said, "I want you to ask yourself that one question again, Stephen, you know the one," as he held his three fingers up in a W: "What would George Washington do?"

That evening when Stephen returned to Boston, he revealed the whole meeting to Jessica. When he finished, Jess said. "Wow, what an honor! You must have been in shock."

"I was," was his reply. "I can see why they want to do it. This country's politics is a mess. It means I have to leave football," replied Stephen.

"Well, you've always said you want to quit while you're on top… No question, you're on top, and this may just be the right time. But my sweet husband and lover, this is a decision only *YOU* can make. I am one hundred percent on your side whichever you choose, and again I say whichever you choose will be the right decision." Jessica declared.

"I don't know the first thing about organizing a new party, let alone running for the office of the President," Stephen exclaimed.

"You'll learn. That's why you'll need Uncle Zack, and of course, with your grandfather overseeing everything, it gives him a reason to get excited, and when that happens, there is nothing that can stop him!"

"Our lives will drastically change, Jess."

"I can say I know that, Stephen, but I really don't. Not until I experience it. Is it a big job to take on? The answer is yes. Will you need help? Lots. But with the resources you have, it can be done. Do you want to be President?" Jess asked.

"That's the question, isn't it?" Stephen replied, then said: "Well, let's write down everything we know and everything we don't, as a start, and determine if it is feasible." And they did, all that night.

The following week the three men once again met. Stephen spoke first. "Before we start, I wish to remind you that a decision will be made within a week from today, one day before my contract renewal negotiations begin." They nodded, and he continued. "And this meeting is to understand what will be involved in this monumental task."

"Yes," replied Jason and continued. "I think we all agree that no commitment will be made today. Let's call today discovery day, shall we? And hope that we all have a true understanding of the depth of this vision. How do you want to do this? Should it be recorded, or will written notes suffice?"

Stephen answered, "I think my written notes will be fine."

They began. The meeting went on for hours, and only half the questions had been answered. The meeting had to be continued the next day until Stephen felt complete in his quest to fill his inexperience and knowledge in the working of an election campaign. The overall plan was broken into two major phases: the first year was to organize a grassroots movement and the second year was to campaign.

Before departing, Stephen had a big last question on his mind that he needed to ask. He said, "Why do you think it has been so difficult to establish a third party in this country?"

Zack and Jason looked at each before Jason replied. "I also asked the same question, and I thought, well, no third party has ever had a knowable, popular, or charismatic person running for President, except maybe Teddy Roosevelt. He left the Republican Party to become nominee for President with the Progressive, Bull Moose Party. He was popular enough, but he lacked a strong political base.

The only *truly* independent person who ever became President was George Washington!"

Chapter XXXV

Mike Glen, the small-time sportscaster/journalist for Russell Prep Football Division, was aggressive as they come. Because of Russell Prep's undefeated season with Stephen as quarterback four years ago, he suddenly became noticed, and by the time Stephen was becoming a star running back for Harvard, Mike had come a long way up the Boston area sportscaster latter and was on his way to national TV. The first time he viewed Harvard's roster, he noticed the name Stephen Kellogg and his finger stopped at the name. He called in his junior reporter, Jenkins, who was assigned to the Harvard games, and asked him, "Do you know anything about this freshman Harvard player, Stephen Kellogg?"

"Not really," he answered. "I think he is older and was in the army. Nobody knows much about him except he is a walk-on," the junior remarked.

"Thanks, see what else you can find on him. I'll do some checking around too. The name sounds familiar," replied Mike.

A week later, Jenkins knocked on Mike's door with information on Kellogg. "Okay, this guy is a 6'8" monster. He's a running back this year, but he's really a qua…"

"Don't tell me," interrupted Mike, "a quarterback. Now I remember," as he turned his head toward the outside window of his office.

"Once I found out he went to Russell Prep four years ago, I thought you would remember him," replied the reporter.

"Yes, and what a quarterback. I lost track of him. I wondered what had happened to him. So now he's a running back. I'll bet he'll be the quarterback next year. Let's learn more about him and how he got so big and good. As I remember, he was an extremely quiet and private person. It was difficult to get any information because he always had someone around protecting him. Try to get an interview with him by going through Coach O'Brien. I think there's a big story behind this kid. I just got a feeling."

"We're only six games into the season, and you're asking me if we are good enough to win the division title. Well, we're going to give it our best shot. We have the talent this year to do it," replied O'Brien.

"And what about that new freshman running back, Kellogg? Where did he come from?" asked Jenkins.

"Kellogg? He was a highly referred walk-on who was coached by George Brown, and we are grateful to have him. He 'll be a star player in his own right, I'm sure of it. Other than that he went to Russell Prep and spent four years in the army; I couldn't tell ya. Oh yeah, I almost forgot, he had no mother or father," said O'Brien.

"Was he an orphan?" asked Mike.

"You might say that, but I know he has some kind of family," replied O'Brien. "Do you mind if Mike Glen or I interview him?"

"No, but only if he agrees to the interview."

"So may I contact him directly about it?"

"Sure, but he has a very private number, so use his e-mail. Tell him to let me know his decision before contacting you about the interview."

"Thanks, coach."

The next day, Stephen called O'Brien after receiving Glen's e-mail.

"Just answer his questions to the best of your knowledge. If you don't know an answer to his question, just say: *I don't know*, and move on to the next question. I know this is your first interview but don't panic. There will be many, many, more. You don't have to say anything about your private life, just football and the team. Keep the answers simple and short, and you'll do fine," said O'Brien.

"Okay, coach, I will let him interview me, and thanks for the advice."

They met at Glen's broadcasting studio one evening after practice. After the cordial introductions of meeting Mike's camera crew, Stephen was led to the interview seating area where Mike's makeup artist did some work on both men and said to Mike, "All set to go."

"Thank you," said the host, then turned toward Stephen and said, "Okay, Stephen, this show is taped and edited, so, if you have to or want to stop at any time, just hold up your hand like this and the cameraman will stop the camera. Make yourself as comfortable as possible and just relax."

Stephen sat there with butterflies in his stomach. It didn't matter how much football he played. It didn't matter how many Special Forces missions he went on; he was nervous; no matter what the host said, he was nervous!

As soon as the camera started rolling, Mike introduced himself and his guest, Harvard's freshman running back, Stephen Kellogg, to his viewers. The very first question that Mike asked Stephen was: "Did you know I watched you play quarterback when you were at Russell Prep? That I was the assistant broadcaster for the team? Stephen was stunned!

"Ah...no...I...didn't." Stephen's face turned red. He was embarrassed that he knew nothing about Mike Glen being a Russell Prep broadcaster. "I apologize for that. I was only fourteen when I started and lived off-campus, so I never really got involved with any of that stuff," said Stephen.

"Oh, please don't apologize. I want to ask you how you wound up at Harvard and if you are happy with the coach and team." Stephen answered the question and all the obvious questions in a good positive fashion until Mike started asking him some things about his past. "You know there were so many times I tried to catch you after a game, and you would disappear. I really wanted to know where you learned football. Can you tell me now?"

Stephen hesitated and thought for a moment and said, "Well, basically, I learned to play football from a coach named George Brown. I was one of his students." And when Mike asked what happened after Stephen graduated from Russell Prep and why he didn't go to college or professional football, Stephen just said: "I wanted to complete my service to my country and was fortunate enough to play football in the army."

The interview never went deeper into his personal life. And when it was over, Stephen felt a sigh of relief and shook hands with everyone while thanking them.

Mike Glen had many other responsibilities than devoting much time to finding out why Stephen H. Kellogg was not a normal football player. But it was always bugging him, and so, when Stephen started playing and winning a lot of games and getting himself a name, Glen made the time and told Stephen he was writing an article for his sports magazine and wanted a private interview to talk about how he came to be a two-handed throwing quarterback which allowed Mike an opportunity to talk about Stephen's past. During the interview, after formalities and discussing some football statistics and seeing Stephen comfortable, Glen said, "You're married with a wife and two children of your own, you live in Boston, and of course, we all know you from playing at Harvard. But where did you grow up?"

After a moment, "I grew up in rural Georgia until I was seventeen," Stephen replied.

"You don't talk like a country boy," said Glen, smiling. "I know you went to Russell Prep when you were fourteen, but where did you play football before that? Did you play at a public or private school?" asked Mike.

"I was home schooled and played in the Pop Warner Leagues where George Brown coached. I was fortunate enough to have him as a coach throughout my life," answered Stephen.

"I understand that you lost your parents right after you were born. Who brought you up? My grandfather lost his wife, my grandmother, in the same accident as my parents, so he raised me in his house."

"Wow! What a blow to your grandfather!" Mike said as he shook his head.

"Yes, it seems he wanted and was able to devote seventeen years of his life to me so that I could become a professional football player. My grandfather always encouraged football and education, and I was taught by the best people." Stephen proudly expressed.

"So it was your grandfather that led you to football?"

"Oh yes, I think the very first mobiles in my crib were footballs. I played other sports too, but my love of the game of football never wavered. Then at seventeen, after graduating from Russell, you disappeared. Would you like to tell us about that?"

"Well, I decided to enlist in the army for service to our country before attending college, to complete my obligation before furthering my education and football career. I had already decided to practice every chance I got, and I was able to play on some army teams," replied Stephen.

"I can't imagine someone not noticing how big, tall and large you are. Were you and are you now on a particular diet? What do you eat?"

After a moment of thought, Stephen said, "I have been and remain on natural healthy food. I learned about nutrition from my grandfather and developed good eating habits, measured by nutritional value, not taste."

When the interview was over, Mike said to Stephen, "Your grandfather was a tremendous influence in your life. I'm sure my readers would be interested in seeing his side. Would you mind if I had a follow-up article with an interview with your grandfather, and what's his name?"

Stephen hesitated, then said, "My grandfather is a very private man. I would have to talk with him personally before I give out any information. I'll let you know."

Chapter XXXVI

As Stephen entered the house through the front door of Jason's home, everyone in the living room stood, anxiously waiting to hear about Stephen's conversation with the Patriots' owners. As the door came wide open and Stephen saw everyone standing, he said, "Oh my gosh, it's only me!" Everyone laughed as he was led into the living room by Jason. The room now held four inner circle members and their wives of the new third party: Jason and Julia Davies, Zachary and Priscilla Blankhardt, Desmond and Cheryl Blankhardt, and Stephen and Jessica Kellogg.

After all the greetings and everyone was seated, Jason invited Stephen to relate the events of this extraordinary day. Stephen began. "All their reactions that we expected occurred. The owners were shocked at the news. And when asked the question about my future plans, I said I'm taking time off to be with my family and help my aging grandfather take care of his affairs. I may come back, but right now, I need this time off. Everything came across just as we planned. The owners and I discussed the quarterback situation, and I gave them my opinion about the two great quarterbacks they have available, so they're going to be alright. Tomorrow will be my big announcement about my retirement. So that's it in a nutshell. Today seemed surreal.

Things seem so different now that it's out. It's like a dream, and I'm still not sure it's not."

At that point, the cook came out announcing that dinner was ready to be served, after which Jason declared, "Tomorrow morning, our work will begin and will officially be the first day of the founding of our third party. Now, let's have dinner and celebrate!"

All the thoughts, meetings, planning, and effort everyone had previously invested in forming a new third party prior to Stephen's official departure from football were made by seven members of the inner circle without Stephen ever knowing. It was very important for Jessica to maintain her normal life while she did legal work for the new party, without Stephen suspecting anything, as she did not want to influence his decision about running for President. Unbeknownst to Stephen, the inner circle, minus him, had met months before Jason asked Stephen to run for President. The future birth of their third party depended totally on Stephen's response.

All the family and guests stayed at the compound that night and the following morning. The meeting started right after breakfast as they watched the large TV screen for the Patriots' owners to announce Stephen's sabbatical from football. This time eight inner circle members attended, and the first order of business was to inform and explain to

Stephen their reason for their previous meetings without him. And while Jason was giving Stephen an explanation, Stephen smiled as he peered into Jessica's eyes as if to say, "You little devil, you were part of this scheme."

There were many questions Stephen had asked at his second meeting, but there were two things Stephen insisted on before he agreed to run for President. First, there was to be *no use of negative ads whatsoever*. Stephen said, "Desperate people use negative methods to cover their shortcomings and insecurity. Negative ads are designed to make voters feel bad to spark the emotion of anger, and that's where further division roots its ugliness. It's the worst kind of political ad. I hope our party lets the voters know the positive actions we can take to bring our country closer by negotiation, which means bending our principals, ideals, or needs for the country's sake." Jason and Zack shook their heads in agreement. "And second, since the three of us have already agreed that the amounts we are donating to the campaign are sufficient to meet all our commitments, estimating that no other funds are required, I would like to propose that we accept *a maximum of $100 donation per donor*, so that we show voters there is no 'influence' money being accepted for favors, and that these donations be used for our party's states' congressional candidates." Once again, all were in agreement.

Immediately after the Patriots made their announcement, Stephen's cell phone started ringing. The very first call was Mike Glen.

"Hi Mike," Stephen said into the phone. "What's this about a sabbatical from football? You didn't sign with the Patriots?" said Mike astounded. "Your contract was going to be history-making. I still cannot believe what I heard. What's going on? What are you going to do?" asked Glen.

"My time is over. For now, I've got family and my aging grandfather to consider. I'm going to cool it for a while and see what other opportunities are available," Stephen answered.

Still believing that Stephen's life story was missing something he couldn't put his finger on, he asked, "Do you think now I can meet your grandfather?" Mike inquired.

"I don't see why not. You'll have to come out to his place, though; he doesn't get out much."

Two weeks after the announcement, Mike Glen met Jason Davies, the man who made Stephen Kellogg into one of the greatest football players ever. Once Glen got Jason Davies' name, he researched all he could to find out what kind of man he was going to meet. He couldn't find much. Jason *was* a private man. He did find the fact that Jason did the research for the government in his specialty of nutrition but not much more. He was disappointed in the limited information he had, and now he wanted to know more. He was not going to be afraid to ask this man tough questions. When Mike Glen arrived at Jason's compound, he was in disbelief. He had never seen anything like it, ever! While driving into the estate, the security alone would impress you. "Who is this guy?" thought Glen as he was led to Jason's office by one of the staff, who then knocked on the door and introduced him.

"Please come in," Jason announced. As soon as Mike entered the room, Jason got up from his desk chair, greeted him with a handshake, and said, "Welcome, Mr. Glen. Please have a seat."

"Thank you for seeing me, Mr. Davies. I had no idea of the magnitude of this estate. How long have you been here?" Glen asked.

"Oh, I guess since Stephen was born some thirty-seven years now. I can't believe I'm in my eighties; it goes by so fast." Jason responded softly.

"Mr. Davies, I'm going to be frank with you and get right to the point. Would that be alright?"

"I don't see why not; go right ahead."

"Now that I am here and have a sense of how Stephen grew up, it tells me a lot."

"Well, young man, I am not ashamed of what I have worked for, and I am grateful for what has been

214

accomplished with Stephen ever since we lost our family that dark day." Jason paused and asked Mike if he would like a drink of some kind; Mike said he was fine and continued with another question.

"Are you upset or concerned that Stephen decided to take a sabbatical from football after all you have done for him to play in the NFL?" queried the broadcaster.

"Not at all," said Jason, "I give counseling when asked, but it was his decision to make."

"Do you know why?"

"I can't answer that question. It's a personal decision on his part."

"Do you know why he left so abruptly?"

"Well, I know his contract was coming up, and he wanted to give the Patriots enough time to adjust to a new quarterback and not leave them empty-handed," Jason explained.

"On another subject, Mr. Davies, when I learned you were Stephen's grandfather, I tried to find some information about you and discovered that there is very little information out there, yet being here and what I see, you must have been an extremely successful man. How is it that there is very little information about you? You're not related to the Great Gatsby, are you?" Mike said jokingly.

Jason laughed and answered, "No, not that I know of. Do you mind telling me about yourself? I read you were a notable nutritionist." Jason nodded. "Is that one of the reasons why Stephen is so big and powerful because you were so strict with his diet, and he started working out at such an early age?" Mike waited for a response.

"Stephen is the result of all the hard work he has put in and all the sacrifices made to accomplish what he had to do to become a star football player. I provided him with a meticulous diet to build and strengthen his body."

"Was there any particular formula you gave him, like growth hormones?"

"Not per se," responded Jason, "I gave some herbs and other natural ingredients, but no unauthorized banned unnatural products. He had to pass all those drug tests to play football. It had to be something that didn't harm his systems, and it was."

"The only article I could find on you was one where you were hired by the US Army to do a nutrition study. Can you tell me a little about that?"

"I really cannot because it was top secret," Jason said.

"Did you use the information you acquired from that study to formulate your diet for Stephen?" asked Mike.

"Well, yes and no," answered Jason. "Once you have learned something, well, you've learned it, and if you use it in combination with other knowledge acquired before or after, it changes the parameter of things. So yes, I did learn a lot at my job doing the study, but it's about putting everything together and making it work properly with other learned knowledge to get successful results. It's not only to have the information but what to do with it," exclaimed Jason.

"Do you consider Stephen to be a normal human being, I mean physically?"

"Yes, I do," replied Jason.

"Don't you think you have created an artificial body?" said Mike.

"Artificial?" repeated Jason.

"Do you feel because you practically programmed Stephen's life and fed him a 'weird scientific diet' that he artificially grew?"

"What kind of question is that?" asked a perturbed Jason and said, "If you feed a kid processed food all his life, is he artificial?"

"My last question, Dr. Davies, did you do all this just so Stephen could play professional football? Was that the main reason?"

Chapter XXXVII

After Stephen accepted their offer, he learned about the other members and was surprised to learn the level of confidence they had in him, making him feel much better about his decision to run for President. A lot of preparation work had already been started, and all the members had already accepted their positions, duties, and responsibilities, which Stephen had not been privy to but would soon learn. Jason was to serve as CEO in charge of the overall planning, execution, finance, and security. Wife Julia would assist Jason in all the administrative functions and act as party secretary. Zachary had total responsibility for building the party at its grassroots and running the campaign with his son Desmond as his deputy, with wives Priscilla and Cheryl assisting their husbands in developing a campaign strategy, a name for the new party media advertising, and marketing materials. Jessica was in charge of legal, starting with the charter and by-laws, speech writing, managing Stephen's schedules, researching and preparing lists of candidates for cabinet and other top government positions, and educating her husband concerning those positions. And for Stephen, in the first year, he was to just 'get out there' and let the country meet him. However, after he officially accepts the nomination from the party to run for President, he will be in charge of delivering the party's message throughout the country and the world.

At one of the inner circle meetings, it was decided that there would be no mention of any candidate's name for one year. The party would be created and established based on its beliefs before selecting a person to run for President. At the beginning of the second year, the year of the election, the candidates, wherever running for office throughout America, will be announced and the respective campaigns will begin. At that meeting, Jason spoke about keeping Stephen's presidential intentions absolutely secret. Many of the political friends that Zachary will approach to determine if they're interested in joining and helping this new party may very well assume that he will be the candidate for President. "That's okay; they can assume whatever they want to. And should anyone inquire about that prospect, Zack's answer is that he has not yet made a decision. When we are established as a viable organization, a year from now, when we want to make our grand entrance into the political arena, please understand that we want Stephen's nomination for President and Zachary as Vice-President to be a complete surprise to the nation." The purpose of this secrecy was to give Stephen time to quietly become a guest speaker on media shows and at such places as universities, military organizations, and medical conventions without the media and political opposition overwhelming his audiences.

Absolutely no political messages were to be delivered until his announcement to run. Stephen's job in the first year would be to introduce himself to the population based on the success of his military and football careers by sharing his life story and experiences via guest speaking. After one year, the topic of his speeches would dramatically change.

The work performed in the inner circle's first year was exciting and exhausting. The Blankhardt family, having the biggest responsibility for organizing the party, a monumental task, would need a big staff of paid personnel plus volunteers. They knew that once it became generally known that a third party was being organized, all the publicity would begin, all the questions would be asked, and all the 'stories' would start. So as softly as they could step, they began hiring and filling in their management supervision staff positions immediately, who then were responsible for hiring and supervising their own staff and volunteers. Repeating the same steps each time a new state, city, or county party headquarters was established. Little by little, starting with disgruntled independent voters inquiring about the new party, joining as a volunteer, and then spreading the news to their families, friends, and neighbors, the unknown, unnamed new party slowly grew. After six months, the inner circle was happy with the progress that had been made, but there was a long, long way yet to go. The plan for the Blankhardt family during that time was to refuse interviews, guest speeches and avoid publicity. After that period, things changed, and as designed, Zachary started accepting invitations for interviews on major national TV and radio stations and social media. The inevitable question, "Are you going to run for President?" was always asked. Each time, true to form, Zachary would answer that he had not decided, but a decision would be made in a few months. The Blankhardt family spent the latter part of the year creating as much of a 'buzz' about the party as they dreamed up. More and more inquiries kept coming in, and by the end of the first year, the party, still without its name but often called The New Party or The Third Party, began to take hold.

Meanwhile, Stephen's first six months were quite different. Stephen and Jessica sold their house in Boston and moved back into Jason's estate compound for security reasons for the family and because the children could be educated and cared for by Grandma Rachael while Jessica worked full time with Stephen, plus the estate was home to the national headquarters for the party. Stephen had existing commitments to companies under contract he represented in national advertising promotions. He continued to meet those obligations while traveling around the country, giving interviews on national networks, speaking at football and veterans organizations, visiting children's hospitals and senior homes, and any other organizations that were unpolitical on their surface. Stephen was to remain far away

221

from the 'buzz' and limelight so that it appeared he had no connection to the party. His speaking engagements were light and fun, never with political views. At this point, everything was low-key, just as it was supposed to be. This went on non-stop the whole year. Whenever he could, while speaking all over the country, Stephen loved to visit with old friends from the army and football days. If it got around that he was visiting someone or attending a football game, there was usually local media coverage, increasing his popularity.

Chapter XXXVIII

It was now time, one year later. A weekend convention in Boston was planned to formally announce to the Nation the formation of a new political party and on the last day of the convention, present the nomination of their candidate for President and Vice-President.. Boston was chosen because of its historic American revolutionary background and fit perfectly with their announcement of their party name. In the first year of their effort to break through the stigma of a viable third party in America, the inner circle did beyond their expectations. Before the convention started, they had recruited thousands of members and volunteers and were pleased. But after the convention, they would need millions. Could it be done?

"Good evening, my fellow party members, invited guests, members of the press, and America. My name is Zachary Blankhardt. Some of you may have already known me as a senator with another party at another time. We are excited to be gathered here today to present to the United States of America a new political party, and that new party will elect a candidate to run for the office of President of our great country. It has taken a tremendous amount of courage and sacrifice by many, many devoted people for me to be here tonight, and I want to give recognition to all those involved. But tonight is the real beginning. Tonight we come out of our shells, tonight is our birth night, and it's time to celebrate. Without waiting any longer, please let me introduce my son, Desmond Blankhardt, who will announce our party's name." As he spoke, he turned toward Desmond with his hand and arm extended, welcoming him to the podium and microphone. "Please welcome Desmond." There was thunderous applause.

After introducing himself, recognizing others, and speaking a few words, Desmond was ready. Two huge banners, one on each side of the stage, were to drop on signal upon Desmond's announcement. "My fellow party members and all of America, I present to you the GWP, the George Washington Party." And with that, down came one banner with large letters GWP, in red, white, and blue, respectively. On the other banner was a large full picture of George Washington with an eagle perched on his arm sleeve, standing between a smaller picture of a donkey with its rear legs up in a kicking position, and on the other side, a rendering of an elephant facing the donkey with its trunk and tusks pointing up. It was created to look like a 'referee' between two fighters. With music blasting, the convention went crazy with cheers and applause, then some of the conventioneers started cheering 'USA, USA, The GWP is A-OK', which spread like wildfire through the masses. After the enthusiasm settled down, the by-laws were read and approved along with other business, and once concluded, Desmond announced that at tomorrow's session, the board would present their final nominations for President and Vice President, after which a vote would be held. The celebration went on and on that night and was considered by the media to be a great success. The next evening, the last day had even more mystery and excitement in it. The new GWP members had no idea what was about to happen. Word got out that Zachary may not be the nominee for President, and the rumor spread so that everyone was guessing who the nominee might be. That's what created the new excitement, the unknown!

The next day with the convention hall filled with an excited and anxious audience, it would be Desmond that makes the historic announcement. "And now, before we present and bring out our candidate for President, who will be escorted on stage with our Vice-President nominee, I would like to introduce some facts about our proposed candidate. First, he has had a high level of education. He's able to understand and speak fluently in seven different languages. He volunteered his service to this country in the US Army, serving as a Special Forces Ranger on 22 missions, earning a Silver Star for his brave actions during one of those missions. After completing his four years of service with the army rangers, he was accepted to and graduated from Harvard University, near the top of his class.

While serving in the army reserves for four additional years as a ranger instructor, he continued his education and received a master's degree in American history."

Desmond stopped. Up till now, it was relatively quiet in the hall. His tone was assuring and calm. Now the words would build. "And after college, this man you are about to meet," and his words became louder and faster, "became one of the greatest football quarterbacks of all time. Please meet our nominee candidate for the President of the United States," and at the same time Desmond was saying, "Stephen H. Kellogg," the back curtain opens, the band starts to play and out walk Stephen and Zachary. It took ten minutes for the hall to quiet down. At first, the men waved and mouthed, 'Thank you'. After a few minutes, with the thundering applause still going on, the two men looked at each other with great big smiles on each of their faces, and for a few moments, they really didn't know what else to do! So they just stood there with smiles waving to their jubilant audience. The reception was beyond their wildest dreams.

Finally, Stephen took the podium. The room grew quiet. People were still standing when he said, "Please be seated. Zachary and I would like to thank you for that warm reception. It is a privilege to be here tonight with you to be part of this historic moment. What a perfect match for President and Vice-President, Zachary for the brains and well...I guess...me the brawn." There was laughter. "They say behind every good man is a good woman. I'd like to introduce our wives, Jessica and Priscilla." At that announcement, the crowd again came to their feet, applauding and cheering while the wives kissed their husbands and took their seats on stage. After everyone was again seated, Stephen continued. "Good evening, my fellow Americans! In all of our country's more than two-hundred-year history, there has never been a successful third party. Maybe it's because there has never been such a greater need than before now. And this may be the time. Because now, it appears the extremes are controlling both the Democratic and Republican parties' thinking, and are flooding the media with lies, hostile rhetoric, and uncompromising proposals with the result of Congress getting little done for the people of this country." A big round of applause and cheering. "The GWP was created for voters who see this country as having and accepting differences, yes, many, many differences. Differences have been with us ever since our nation was born. Even Native American Indians had differences. AMERICA, THAT'S WHO WE ARE! The good people of this country accept and thrive on freedom's differences. There is no other country like America. This party wants to attract voters who want Congress to pass legislation that's good for the country, NOT THEIR PARTY. We shall be the voice of REASON! As we grow stronger, we can be the balance, buffer, and wedge between the other two parties.

And as we do that, we reduce the power of extremist thinking and get our country back to our principles of freedom for everyone. Let me take a moment to tell you how we decided on our name GWP. When I was just a little boy, my grandfather said, "Stephen, we are all caring for you as best as we can as substitute parents, but I cannot replace the father you will never have. So, I was thinking what a great idea if we read about the father of our country, George Washington, to see how he was raised as a boy to become our First President." He handed me my first book on George Washington, and he read it to me every night. Ever since then, I have read everything I could find about this great man. I had truly come to know, love, and respect him. The kind of person I would want as my father. After I was offered the opportunity of being the party's nominee, I was overwhelmed with emotions and needed time to let this monumental decision sink in and think things through. Understanding my position, my grandfather asked me, "Stephen, what would George Washington do? As many of you may know, I have gone to school, played football, and lived and raised my family right here in Boston, where it all began for our nation. I feel very much attached to its history. In the beginning, we were a collection of separate colonies that George Washington and our founding fathers knew could only win independence by unifying those colonies. The representatives of the colonies negotiated and reasoned their way into unification. Today we offer our GWP to any and all who want to join in that original spirit of Freedom: life, liberty, and the pursuit of happiness, for all our citizens. Next year, before the elections, Zachary and I will visit all of our great country to deliver our party's message. We can do it! We can rise up to become a factor for good, sensible government conducted with dignity. America, we love our freedom, don't let the extremes push out rationale and negotiation from our government. Bring back the spirit of unification to accomplish our country's goals. May our Creator bless this United States of America and keep us safe. Thank you all, and good night." All four were at center stage while the cheering and applause were thundering through the convention hall as the band started playing the song, Good Times Are Just Around The Corner!

Long before the convention, the massive undertaking of spreading the party's grassroots had already started. The Blankhardts and Jessica had begun preparing lists and lists of people acquired from all the members of the Inner Circle. The initial lists were filled with names with whom Stephen had made a connection over the years of his life. As he had learned from his Grandfather and Coach Brown all through his youth, "Be friendly, smile, make friends." The lists included famous football players and other sports greats and broadcasters, army friendships and Harvard alumni, and many, many friends and fans. Then the lists acquired from

229

the others of the Inner Circle were composed of everyone they could think of. From its start, it grew slowly and quietly, as was predicted, but after the televised convention, it grew geometrically. Millions of Americans had watched to see who would be the presidential candidate of the new GWP. That following morning, Stephen's imposing size, charismatic personality, and seemingly easy delivery of his words was the number one story headlined on all the news stations and newspapers and was the topic of most Americans all that day. Never before had there ever been a third-party candidate that had so much previous popularity throughout the nation before the campaigning began. The day after the convention, the headlines were blasting the name **Stephen H Kellogg** all over the country. There would be nothing public for a few days. This was the time needed to prepare for the campaign. It had been a year since building a grassroots organization and today was the first day to lead this organization to become fully grown. Now the cat was out of the bag. The party had a name, GWP, a logo with George Washington in it, and a well-known affable candidate for President. The energy was high!

Chapter XXXIX

At the GWP Compound Headquarters, Jason sat at the head of the large mahogany conference table. Julia sat on the left side of the table, with Stephen and Jessica seated on the right side. At the other end of the conference table, facing directly opposite Jason, was Zachary, seated and surrounded by the other members of his family. Jason opened the meeting. "First, I want to congratulate and thank all of you for the great success of bringing this dream of a GWP to American voters. This alone is a tremendous accomplishment. We all should be very proud to represent a political organization based on reason. Well, I hope everyone was able to get some sleep, as our next step to get our people elected will require even more effort than ever before. Let's start our meeting with brief summary reports of the next actions to be taken. Zachary, please reveal our readiness for this campaign. Thank you, Jason. Well, briefly, Priscilla has been working with Jessica to set our schedules over this next year so that we are speaking in different parts of the country simultaneously without overlapping. I will be emphasizing *balance* in our political system as we have in our government. I will let the voters know and understand that policies should stand like palm trees, able to bend amid strong winds but not breaking, that is, accomplishing legislation through the winds of negotiation. And, while

231

Priscilla and I are touring the nation, I will inform the voters why I have enthusiastically embraced the GWP..." He paused a moment, faced Desmond, and said, "Desmond and Cheryl, if I may..." they nodded yes, "will be manning the National Headquarters. Desmond has installed direct lines to all fifty state headquarters' chiefs, which will provide almost instantaneous instructions and assistance to them. Cheryl will contact the deputy chief of each location to compile all our statistics, help in planning for the state campaigns and monitor all ads by all the Parties while assisting Desmond wherever necessary."

"Thank you, Zachary. Stephen and Jessica, what are your plans?" Stephen spoke.

"We decided to present the ideals of George Washington, who never really associated himself with a political party but only wanted to unite the colonies into a federal government. Each of my speeches will carry a story about our revolution. I will bring up the fact that this country has had many different political parties in the past and that even the two major parties today came from remnants of other parties, that change can be good for progress, and that a major change in politics, going from a two-party system to a three-party system, is what our country now needs. Jessica is helping me with my speeches to convey these messages to our voters." Stephen turned to Jessica to allow her to speak. "I have drafted a schedule for the forthcoming year for

Stephen. Our first step with the exclusive Mike Glen interview played extremely well with the viewing audience and got commendable ratings. Kicking off the campaign, Stephen will guest on the national political talk shows on Sundays, starting this coming Sunday. From there, we will start traveling, first to Boston. We intend to spend one five-day week in each state. The schedule for each stop throughout the country will basically be the same: Appear on local TV stations, visit our state GWP Headquarters and a local public school in the mornings, attend a lunch speaking engagement, then in the afternoon, pay a visit to a business, veterans or social organization group. Evening events have been planned for two major speaking engagements at major colleges, and the remainder of the nights and weekends are for future guest invitations for TV and other media appearances. Two weeks before we visit each college, our staff of volunteers will be calling everyone we know who went to that school to invite them and their families to be our guests at the event. As planned, the campaign will stop one week before the election. Of course, as we move along and evaluate our situation, there will be changes, but for now, our objectives and course will be as presented. Thank you, Stephen and Jessica." Jason took back the floor and turned to Julia for a financial report. She gave her analysis of the campaign finances and how and when monies would be distributed to the national and local headquarters and gave her opinion about the future expenses. When she had finished, Jason asked for questions or comments, and when that was concluded, the meeting ended with the Inner Circle excited and ready to move ahead with their enormous tasks. It started out with a lot of enthusiasm and spirit, but it became non-stop exhaustion every day. The more events, the greater the popularity and the increased requests for personal appearances. It was working, but everyone was paying the price. Keeping up the pace and keeping a high level of enthusiasm and positivism in the campaign was challenging.

"Do you see this glass of water I am holding up?" Stephen answered a question after speaking to the crowd in a large auditorium in Ohio. It had been six months that had already passed. Stephen tried to avoid too much repetition in his appearances and talks. If there was enough time remaining at the end of Stephen's speech, questions were taken. Here, he was given the question, "What makes your party, the GWP, any different than the other two parties? He wanted to explain heart and perspective. He wondered what he could do or use to explain his answer while peering over the adjacent guest table to the right of the podium. He leaned over, picked up a water glass from the table, and poured a little water out of one glass into the other one sitting nearby, making it look as close as possible to half full. Then holding up the glass in his left hand, asking his question to the student while always remembering to bring humor at every opportunity, he continued speaking while pointing his right finger at the glass. "If I turn this glass of water upside down and the water stays in the glass, will you believe our party is different?" while everyone was laughing, he said, "Just kidding! But look, you may not be able to see clearly enough from that distance, but the water in this glass is about halfway to the top. You can view this same glass of water in two opposite ways. We believe part of the problem that our opponents are experiencing is that they see this glass as half empty. The members we have and want in our GWP see this glass as half full. We want to show the positive side of actions to be taken instead of the negativism inherent in the words, *half empty*. We want to show America our position on approaching and solving issues.

Another major important aspect of our differences is that we neither enlist nor will support extremists. We believe negotiation is crucial in accomplishing goals and is the key to passing legislation. Extremists dislike negotiation because they don't get everything they want. And lastly, we are a party that is based on the ideals and principles of The Father of Our Country with a belief in asking ourselves, "What would George Washington do? I wish to thank you, sir, for that question and thank this college administration for allowing us the opportunity to be here with you tonight. I believe…" turning to Jessica who was sitting at the podium guest table pointing to her watch, "…my boss is telling me that we have run out of time, so thank you for coming out this evening and having an open mind just to listen to our story. Our volunteers are in the lobby, should you have a further interest in the GWP. May our Creator bless us and this wonderful country we live in. Thank you, America. Good night." There was a standing ovation as he left the stage.

On another occasion, as a guest on a round table news media show, when Stephen was asked for his opinion about the attack on the Capital Building years ago, he responded, "I think it was George Washington's words that stated: *Beware of the false Patriot.* The language one uses, such as words and body language that can convey mixed meanings as well as the tone of the oration, might spark a reaction in an ugly form. Politicians use words created by their clever writers for such purposes. **Words matter!** Even telling someone to MARCH on something may imply anger or danger. *Oh, let's take it further; After words like, you have to fight for what you want.* Now, you're not too far away from the word, ATTACK. It was disgraceful, to say the least. It was bands of thugs being thugs. They could care less about our constitution, bringing weapons and chemicals to ensure that it would be them if there was any violence. You don't bring a weapon to a peaceful demonstration for *protection*! If I am elected President, when I take the oath of office to protect the Constitution of the United States, I'll keep it!" When questioned about federal taxes, he responded, "We are looking into a flat percentage rate for individual filers that will work for all income categories that will be fair. Everyone should pay tax. When we send our fleet out to sea or fly our aircraft in the skies, it is for everyone's protection. A flat percentage rate does away with deductions and a host of other record-keeping activities and makes life's finance's easier and more predictable. The same will apply to corporations and other entities. All profitable businesses must pay tax."

When interviewed on a popular early morning national TV show by an old friend who was an ex-NFL player and now a host, Stephen was comfortable and relaxed. It was a very informal interview, the ones Stephen liked the best. The script was unplanned. The questions were to be about his life. "I'm sure a lot of the audience has seen you guesting on many political shows in the past few months, and many know of your football career and fame, but the question most requested by our listening audience is, Stephen, what was it like for you, growing up?" asked the commentator. "Wow, that's a good one! This is going to seem so ironic because I'm always speaking out against political extremes." They both laughed. "The fact of the matter is, I was brought up in a very loving and protective environment. I was somehow spared, but I lost my parents and maternal grandmother in a horrific auto accident when I was taken home from the hospital right after my birth. I was the first child, so there were no brothers or sisters. My father was raised in an orphanage with no known parents, and I had no one left except one grandfather to raise me. That might not be the average American child's story, but this next part makes it slightly extreme. My grandfather was a noted nutritionist and became wealthy by investing in biotech startups and building a multi-million dollar estate that I grew up on as a boy. I had two female tutors that were my surrogate mothers and a Hall of Fame football coach who taught me football and became the father I never had. All of these people, including our cook Alisa, became my family. I was put on a special diet, received a tutored education, learned to speak several languages, and was brought up with strict study habits and a big emphasis on physical training, especially football. My life was scripted and drilled into me every day, in every way. There was nothing normal about my life. At a very young age, when I first started playing football with other young kids, I realized how sheltered and protected I had been. I was larger than most kids my age, and I learned so much about football that I could relate to the coaches better than my teammates, and so I was a *loner* in the beginning." Stephen paused. The commentator spoke. "What a beginning, unusual to say the least! Did you ever rebel against any of those things that were happening in your

238

life at that time? Not really, because there were future events in my life which helped shape my views," replied Stephen. Once, when I was even younger, I was told I was to visit homeless people living under a bridge. When I asked why, I was informed that I must be able to put myself in someone else's shoes, and that meant feeling what the other person feels. The day before, I was to bring breakfast from a fast food store to these homeless people. I was encouraged, I guess, is the best word, to fast that day, which I did. At the end of the day, after having followed my daily scheduled routine, I felt tired and hungry and went to bed early. The next morning, feeling hungry and having my stomach react in a way I had never experienced, my grandfather, my tutor, and I delivered breakfast acquired from a fast food restaurant and sat there under the bridge with about ten homeless people and heard their stories while they ate. I had always eaten healthy organic food. I had never eaten fast food. My grandfather told me not to eat it because of preservatives, added sugars, and chemicals that were not good for my body. But I was so hungry! I didn't know what to do. My grandfather leaned over to me and said: "It's okay to try it. Don't eat a lot, but know and feel what it's like to live and eat like these people. This is where they live and what they eat almost every day of their lives. The food we eat costs more, and they cannot afford to pay." There was a short pause, after which Stephen continued. "There was one more

239

incident I would like to relate to your viewers if you don't mind, and that is about the day I asked why I had no parents, like other kids. Again, I was very young. Those who were caring and educating me, my family, gathered around me as my grandfather told me the story. The next week, I was taken to an orphanage, similar, I was told, to the one my father had once lived in. I met many boys and girls while I was there and could see the sadness in some of their faces and feel it in my body. And when I got home, I went to my room and cried all night. I began to recognize how blessed I was to have all these people in my life who loved me. And how privileged I was at having all that was given to me. I learned that putting my feet in someone else's shoes was a good lesson to learn."

At an interview done remotely from the GWP Headquarters on a late evening TV news show, the commentator asked Stephen, "What do you say to your opponents when they say you are young and have no political experience? Do you mean, what would I say to them or you? To them" replied the host. Stephen waited a moment and said, "I would say to them, Thank you for that observation." Then, in a moment of silence, he said in a stunned voice, "To me, what would you say to me." Stephen attempted to answer, To you, I would say, "I won't get into the meaning of the word *young* because it's is such a relative term, but it could be age discrimination. But I will say that I am past the age required to run for President, and that's all that should matter. As far as my political experience, they are absolutely right. First, I have no experience..." curtly interrupting Stephen in the middle of the sentence with his next question, the host blurted out something that Stephen didn't hear because he was speaking, so he stopped speaking. When the question ended, there was dead silence, then Stephen said calmly, "I did not understand the entire question because I was still giving you my answer to the prior question you had just asked. But it will not be necessary for you to repeat that question, because I choose not to answer your questions if I cannot give you my complete answers. Therefore with due respect, I bid you good night." Stephen then terminated his remote connection to the show.

The following morning, Stephen's actions were all over headlines and gossip news columns. That same morning he visited a live late morning TV talk show hosted by a panel of five women, with the first question being about the previous night's incident. "What happened? Everyone thinks you walked off the show to get headlines, so could you please let our listeners know why you ended the interview so abruptly?" Stephen answered in his normally calm voice, "I felt disrespected. I don't need to be in the headlines. Just give me a mission to perform, a football to throw, and a country to lead... When I am cut off while giving an explanation, the media is broadcasting only the words they want their listeners to hear, and I will NOT allow the media to speak for me! When I am asked a question, I expect to receive the proper time to give a clear answer, not just Yes or No. Answers like that never give people a chance to ask why he answered *the question that way*? When you answer *why*, your answer gives your reasoning and beliefs. It allows the listeners to get a clearer understanding of the Yes or No answer and who YOU are, and isn't more clarity what we all want? When I speak, I am direct. I use simple words and sentences to be clear and not to be misunderstood. Words are so important! The definition, voice tone and volume, and physical gestures give meaning to a word, but only for that moment. A word may have many meanings and may be interpreted differently because of the circumstances I just mentioned." When Stephen appeared to have finished speaking, one of the other women hosting the show asked him, "When you were interrupted last night, you were about to explain your answer about being inexperienced in political matters and the way things are run in Congress, etc., could you give our listeners today, the answer you wanted to convey last night?" Stephen paused, "What I was about to say was that my opponents are absolutely right about me being inexperienced in political matters. I want all of America to know that I have NO experience in political... bribery, no experience in political corruption, absolutely no experience in political lying, sexual harassment, or insider information stock trading...shall I go on?" They were all

242

laughing when he said, "However, on a more serious note, I did acquire leadership training skills as an Army Ranger Team Leader and Instructor, and I have quarterbacked a professional football team to a few Super Bowl wins, and I have a Vice Presidential Candidate that has spent many, many years in the Senate with similar beliefs, principals and ideas for the future of America, as I have. I think the leadership, knowledge, and experience of the inner workings of Congress is well understood, and we know we are capable of all the responsibilities of leadership of our country. And by the way, political extremists, thugs, and people who hate are not invited to join the GWP. This is a free country, so those types of people can vote for the other candidates." At that point, Stephen was asked to give an example of a political extremist. "Well, on one end of the spectrum is a man with an American Flag, attacking a Capital Police officer at the Congressional Building, which I call, the false patriot, who says he lives by the Constitution and civilized laws. And on the other opposite side, the other extreme, is a man with a rope and a hammer destroying a statue representing our cultural history, with the idea that he can erase or change history." When Stephen was asked the next question to reveal his relationships with the women throughout his life, he spoke extensively about his relationships with his tutors, Rachael and Suzanne, Cook Alisa, and of course, Jessica. He related the story of going to his first chaperoned dance at an all-girls school and a funny story about girls when he was in prep school. He mentioned that after prep school, he enlisted in the army, and his life was so full that he had little time for romance. But after serving two years, when he went back home on leave and saw Jessica as a woman instead of the little girl he remembered, his heart pounded, and from that moment on, he couldn't stop thinking about her and knew he was in love. When asked about his religious views, he explained. "I am very candid about religion. I believe religion is a very personal private affair, and the wisdom to separate church and state in our constitution is brilliant. This great country has allowed, and hopefully always will allow, religious beliefs to exist and thrive in this country, but not any who preach hate or treason, as actions are always louder than words. We are a country made up of differences. Let's use our differences as if they were assets, and let's invest in them. I come from a Judaeo/Christian ancestry. I have studied religions at Harvard, so I have had some education in that area. I do not prefer to use the word G O D because of its misuse. Once again... words *are* important... I choose personally to believe in a *Creator*. I accept the fact that our existence in the world was created by a Higher Source. I trust in nature, universal balance, and the goodness, whatever amounts, in every human heart. You might say I have a spiritual outlook on life, with respect to all religions that preach and practice love."

There were many interviews and many stories Stephen would tell along his campaign journey. His college rally speeches always had a story about the American Revolution, always emphasizing the tremendous sacrifices made by true Patriots, giving their lives so that we could be here this day, living in freedom. Always spending as much time as he could milling and talking with the people, he was always well received. But along with the fanfare, he had his share of annoyances, people stalking him, accusing him of this or that, but he didn't take any of it to heart. He and Jessica knew very well that these things were going to happen. It was similar to the same nuisances he had experienced in being a famous football star. It bothered everyone close to him, but he remained and appeared unconcerned. He had to stay *up* and keep going. The path was so clear to him. Stephen continued his vigorous campaigning until one week before the election as planned, then suddenly, the election was here. Stephen could feel the tide rising around him. The race was close. The polls indicated that GWP was putting up a strong showing, but as of now, there was no candidate showing enough votes to get elected. There might have to be a run-off election. With just two days remaining, Stephen had his final short speech to make on national TV Monday night, *the night before the election*, at 8:30 PM EST, right before

Monday Night Football. It would be broadcast from a location in Boston, and all eight Inner Circle members would be on stage, along with all the national legislative candidates, for his final message to America.

Chapter XXXX

"My fellow Americans, for those of you who have tuned into this broadcast, I wish to thank you. I know how much you have suffered through these campaign media ads and globs of mail in your mailboxes. It's almost over, so I'll be succinct. We are gathered here in Boston, where the idea of an independent and free nation was born. In the beginning, it was just skirmishes by individual colonies, such as the ones that had occurred in the colony of Massachusetts at Lexington, Concorde, and Bunker Hill. There was no Army or Navy. When George Washington became Commander-in-Chief of the Continental Forces, he had NOTHING! He had to create a military with few arms, little gunpowder, few blankets, and nothing but tattered and shredded clothing worn by a diverse group of men. And with those few assets, they dared to challenge the world's most powerful nation. The war began with a short series of continuous losses and retreats by the Continental Army, discouraging and almost disbanding and destroying it. To save his army, Washington devised a bold plan. With their feet frozen for lack of shoes, and their bodies thin from lack of food, they dragged their cannons on horse-drawn sleds through snow-covered hills & mountains and then had to load the cannons, horses, and men onto barges to cross the Delaware many times, continuously and quietly, through the blistering cold night, then march through a blinding snow blizzard, all under cover of darkness, until they reached their objective, Trenton, on Christmas Eve 1776. The ragged army under George Washington accomplished its *Victory or Death* mission with secrecy and stealth. The surprised enemy of Hessians was overwhelmed, which gave The Continental Army their first victory against a professional army. The military victory had little strategical or tactical significance, but it boosted morale in the country and the army's confidence. But most importantly, that attack, that night, planned and executed by General Washington and his men, showed the country that it had a chance to win its *independence*. The losses, suffering, and the price paid that took place that night just for Washington's army to reach their destination, were horrific. I ask you, have we taken their suffering for granted? Were those Patriots not immigrants themselves or from families of prior immigrants? We should continue to build America with the talents the immigrants bring with them. We need labor to help us grow, fix our battered infrastructure, serve in our military, and become educated to teach others who will help us expand our knowledge in the sciences, medicine, and other industries. We need help with cyber and identity theft rampant throughout our country. Our government agencies are needlessly inundated with reports and complaints concerning financial theft and security breaches. We need to implement strong preventive measures that work! The government is NOT properly protecting us! Protecting its citizens should be its main priority. To assist in this effort, the increased use of fingerprint technology, electronic purchase notifications, and new technology to combat cybercrime must be found and utilized throughout the country. There is so much opportunity in these areas to create jobs while solving those problems. And speaking about solving problems, now is the time to control our natural resources better before any more serious damage can be done. For example, we can help protect our parks and lumber industry by constructing badly needed fire break walls in our forests.

"Another example is our changing weather. Arguing who is right or wrong on whether the environment is being affected by man, nature, or both doesn't solve the problem itself. The problem is the fact that weather patterns appear to be changing, whatever the cause! There are actions on our part that can be and must be taken to counter those changing weather patterns while creating new jobs, such as constructing solar desalination plants to bring water to our farmers, as well as supply desalinated water to our arid deserts, which then opens up new useful land for settling immigrants into new communities by having them build their own homes, farms, and cities there. This is how America flourishes and has always been done with diversity. The American Revolution proved that people of many different religious beliefs, colors, country origins, languages, and occupations can succeed with the same goal, and we can continue to succeed in all our aspirations when our country is able to rally together in agreement... What has happened to that spirit and energy? What kind of behavior is being displayed to our children, our greatest asset, and to the world. Do the politicians in the other two parties serve America? Or is it their *party* that comes first? Are we listening to the words of false patriots, as Washington himself once wrote, while the Colonies were in the midst of forming a new federal government, *Beware of the false patriot!*

We, the GWP, want to counter and calm the mean tone of our political opponents who exploit the media. *We want to break through the self-serving extremists, the false patriots! We* believe the American voter deserves another choice, a party for the sensible, reasonable person, open to sharing with others with love in their heart for all mankind. We believe the word freedom is for every American, not just those who define it with conditions for themselves. Freedom must be extended to each American by each American without fear of prejudice or judgment, and those freedoms must continue to be protected and enforced by our constitution.

"I have posed many questions tonight and given you a lot to think about. It is obvious to us the positions the other two parties have taken. America, this is our chance to break through and take our opponents by surprise, and that's why I am asking for your vote. And so, before you cast your vote in tomorrow's election, ask yourself this question," as he held his right hand up with his three middle fingers in the formation of a **W** and said, *"**What would George Washington do...?** Thank you, America, The blessed land that I love."

THE END